The Musical Genesis of Felix Mendelssohn's *Paulus*

Siegwart Reichwald

The Scarecrow Press, Inc.
Lanham, Maryland, and London
2001

SCARECROW PRESS, INC.

Published in the United States of America
by Scarecrow Press, Inc.
4720 Boston Way, Lanham, Maryland 20706
www.scarecrowpress.com

4 Pleydell Gardens, Folkestone
Kent CT20 2DN, England

British Library Cataloguing-in-Publication Information Available

Library of Congress Cataloging-in-Publication Data

Reichwald, Siegwart, 1967–
    The musical genesis of Felix Mendelssohn's Paulus / Siegwart Reichwald.
        p. cm.
    Includes bibliographical references (p.) and index.
    ISBN 0-8108-4047-2 (alk. paper)
        1. Mendelssohn-Bartholdy, Felix, 1809–1847. Paulus. I. Title.

MT115.M53 R45 2001
782.23—dc21   2001031053

⊖™ The paper used in this publication meets the minimum requirements of
American National Standard for Information Sciences—Permanence of
Paper for Printed Library Materials, ANSI/NISO Z39.48-1992.
Manufactured in the United States of America.

Contents

Examples

Figures

Tables

Acknowledgments

Various institutions have graciously provided the original source material that made this study possible: the Biblioteka Jagiellonska Kraków, the Staatsbibliothek zu Berlin Preußischer Kulturbesitz, the Bodleian Library, the New York Public Library, the Bibliotheque du Conservatoire Royal de Musique Brussels, and the Stanford University Library. My colleague, Werner Mertz, was very kind in helping me produce the figures for this book.

Thanks to Dr. Larry Todd, who gave me access to personal microfilm copies of various manuscripts, to Dr. Jeffrey Sposato, whose transcriptions of the libretto sources were very helpful, and to Dr. Michael Cooper and Dr. Ralf Wehner, for sharing their insights on the subject.

My committee members, Dr. Charles Brewer, Dr. Jeffery Kite-Powell, and Dr. André Thomas were helpful as well as supportive. Special thanks to Dr. Douglass Seaton, who not only gave me the needed guidance throughout this project, but also gave me interest in musicology in the first place.

I am very grateful to my brother Friedhelm, who assisted me on my research trip to Krakow, and to my parents, who spent countless hours reading through Mendelssohn's personal correspondence. Finally, I am most thankful for my wife's continuous support and her countless sacrifices over the past years.

Chapter 1

The Oratorio in the Nineteenth Century and Mendelssohn's *Paulus*

Oratorio Traditions in the Early Nineteenth Century

Contemporaneous Understanding of the Genre

In the first half of the nineteenth century the German oratorio saw tremendous changes in its function, content, performance venues, and musical style. The only element untouched by these changes was its basic formal construction. Two oratorios representing the opposites of this development are Louis Spohr's *Die letzten Dinge* (1825) and Felix Mendelssohn's *Elias* (1847). While only twenty-two years separate these works, and while their tonal language and formal structures are similar, the compositional approach to the genre is completely different.

The libretto of *Die letzten Dinge* was written by Friedrich Rochlitz (1769-1842); it is reflective, lyrical in character. It very well exemplifies Johann Georg Sulzer's definition of oratorio:

> A lyrical and short sacred drama, to be performed with music, for use in a worship service on high feast days. Naming it a lyrical drama signifies that its content is a gradually unfolding story, with actions,

1

intrigues, and complex plots, as is the case in a theatrical play. The oratorio features different characters, who, alone and in a group, express thoughts and feelings about a religious event or idea, which is the object of the celebration. The goal of this drama is to wake similar sentiments in the hearts of the audience.

The content of the oratorio is commonly a well-known subject, of which the feast is a reminder. Consequently, it can be dealt with in a thoroughly lyric fashion, because neither dialogue nor narration, nor reports of what is happening, are necessary. One knows ahead of time the cause of the sentiments, which move the singer, and the circumstances of the setting. All this can be communicated through the expression and content of the singing characters; no actual narration is needed.[1]

Howard E. Smither, in his discussion of the late classical oratorio, points out that this definition obviously sees the oratorio mainly as a lyrical genre; its text is still primarily based on the aesthetic values of *Empfindsamkeit*. While Smither explains that a distinction was made between a lyric and dramatic oratorio, he also shows that the lyric, *empfindsam* oratorio was the one considered modern, and it predominated from the mid-eighteenth century well into the nineteenth century.[2]

One of the main characteristics of Mendelssohn's *Elias* is that it is dramatic. Elijah's heroism is carefully chiseled out throughout the work. Every voice takes part in the action. G. A. Keferstein, in his lectures on the oratorio in 1843, defined the modern oratorio as "the artistically precise, very vivid, dramatic representation of a profound idea in its development from beginning to end carried by the music, without intention or necessity of theatrical representation, in order to achieve its full impression."[3] Keferstein, after having quoted Sulzer's definition earlier in his article, took issue with Sulzer over the dramatic aspect of an oratorio:

> The oratorio, according to Sulzer, is a drama. Agreed! In former times is was just that, a theatrical drama—as we have seen. However, when Sulzer assumes it possible for the "gradually unfolding story" to be portrayed by purely musical means without any theatrical means; when he furthermore wants all action and reaction, catastrophes and resolutions to be banned, then where is the drama? Is not such a drama, the way Sulzer describes it, like a knife without handle and blade? Is there any other choice then for the oratorio but to be mere foggy and hovering reflection, expressed by fuzzy characters, who are lyrical, indeed conceived as highly lyrical? This seems unbearable to anyone![4]

It is interesting to note that Keferstein did not see a move toward dramaticism merely as a new development, he espoused it as a necessity of good oratorio writing:

> Rochlitz himself wrote an oratorio (*Die letzten Dinge*), which, while corresponding to Sulzer's definition and while having been set to wonderfully lyrical music by Spohr, could not gain lasting recognition because of its total lack of dramatic clarity and vitality, however much the sometimes heavenly beautiful music deserves it.
>
> That is exactly how many older and newer works of this type fared. If one asks, however, why it is, that the works of a Handel or Haydn, for example, keep and even gain in popularity, the indisputable reason is that the masters breathed a truly fresh, healthy, dramatic life into the music; while the texts of the poets were often lacking, the composers were able to create this through the power of their genius.
>
> While some recent writers and composers probably recognized what the oratoric genre was lacking, as it sank into a deadly rut, they did not dare to follow courageously their own ideas, solely out of fear of the bugbear of the fundamentally stillborn theory. The most excellent among Schneider's oratorios have already shown numerous welcome traces of a dramatic approach, for which they have continuously been well received by the audience.
>
> Yet closer and clearer to the idea of oratorio conceived as truly pure music drama came Professor Giesebrecht in Stettin (1835 and 1836) in his two oratorios for male voices, *Die eherne Schlange* and *Die Apostel von Philippi*; it was Professor Marx, however, who through his *Moses* was able completely to free the oratorio from its Egyptian captivity of faulty theories, and who pointed it in the right direction, through which it is now in the position of being able to develop freely, richly, and greatly.[5]

Oratorio Composers

Keferstein praises Friedrich Schneider (1786-1853), Carl Loewe (1796-1869), and Adolf Bernhard Marx (1795-1838) as driving forces behind the new development toward a better, dramatic oratorio. Of these three, Loewe is the only composer still well known today, not, however, as a composer of oratorios but as a song composer. This reflects the rapid rise and decline of the oratorio style of the early nineteenth century.

Schneider might exemplify better than any other composer the approach to oratorio composing in the early- to mid-nineteenth century.[6] The Dessau *Kapellmeister* was regarded as the most prominent com-

poser of the genre, having written sixteen oratorios. Many of his oratorios, such as *Höllenfahrt des Messias* (1810), *Weltgericht* (1819-20),
and *Die Sündflut* show the popular apocalyptic themes of the early
nineteenth century. Altough Spohr's *Die letzten Dinge* follows the
same theme as Schneider's *Weltgericht*, the approach is completely different. Spohr's oratorio is reflective, with many solos; Schneider's
Weltgericht consists almost exclusively of dramatic choruses, an ex-
treme Handelian approach. In fact, Schneider was often referred to by
nineteenth-century writers as the "Handel of our time."[7]

Other popular oratorio composers of the time were Bernhard Klein
(1793-1832) and Ferdinand Ries (1784-1838). Klein's approach was
similar to Schneider's, while Ries followed Spohr's models. In the
1830s a noticeable turn away from apocalyptic subjects took place.
Popular composers such as Loewe, Marx, Karl Eckert (1820-79), and
Heinrich Elkamp (1812-68) wrote heroic oratorios based mostly on Old
Testament figures, taking Handel's oratorios as models.[8]

It is important to note that for these composers the oratorio had a
completely different function than for Sulzer's generation of oratorio
composers. During the latter part of the eighteenth century the oratorio
had still been mainly considered a church music genre, with the edification of the congregation as its goal. In the 1830s the oratorio had
moved from the church to the stage, providing musical education for
the members of *Singvereine* and sophisticated entertainment for the audience.

The Rise of Choral Associations and Music Festivals

The tremendous rise of choral associations during the latter part of the
eighteenth century, which was fueled by the decline of the school-
related church choir,[9] aided this shift from the sacred to the secular.
While many concerts of choral associations took place in churches, the
church building was merely a convenient performance setting. Concert
life rather than the church service had become the center of the com-
munity. Choral associations even took the repertoire of the musical
church service out of its context and gave it new, independent life.

The biggest events for choral associations besides their regular
concerts were music festivals, which sprang up all over Germany.
Many composers wrote oratorios for music festivals rather than church
performances. In fact, Schneider wrote almost all of his sixteen oratorios for specific music festivals.[10]

One of the largest and most important music festivals was the Lower Rhine Music Festival, which took place annually beginning in 1818. Cecelia Hopkins Porter, in her article on the Lower Rhine Music Festivals, also points out the centrality of the oratorio in these Festivals.[11] The first Lower Rhine Music Festival consisted of the two Haydn oratorios *Die Schöpfung* and *Die Jahreszeiten*. During the next several years an oratorio was always the main work of each festival. It was usually either a newly composed oratorio or an oratorio by Handel, whose dramatic oratorios had become the undisputed model for this genre. Again, oratorios were written for specific festivals; examples are Klein's *Jephta* in 1827 and Ries's *Sieg des Glaubens* in 1829.

The continuing success as well as the popularity and broad base of the Lower Rhine Music Festivals can be seen in the steady rise in numbers of performers and audiences who participated and attended.[12] Among these performers there were very few professionals—including soloists. Porter observes that "the first fifty years of the Lower Rhine Festival . . . reflect the process by which an expanding, increasingly affluent, enlightened, and urban bourgeoisie acquired control over the musical establishment and provided the substance of a new mass public."[13] The modern, dramatic oratorio clearly reflects that development in its secularization and its increased intention to provide entertainment.

Mendelssohn and the Oratorio Traditions in the Early Nineteenth Century

Mendelssohn's Understanding of the Genre

Felix Mendelssohn's understanding of what makes a good oratorio was different from that of Keferstein, who quite clearly seems to refer indirectly to Mendelssohn's *Paulus* in his warnings against bad oratorio writing:

> For all three types of oratorios there is one main prohibition: boredom, of which the penalty is oblivion; on the contrary, they have to be as lively and stirring as possible.
> Notoriously boring, however, is and must be an oratorio, if it does not establish a main focus, but instead loses itself in vagueness and wavers about in lyricism without a firm core of action, effect, and aspiration based on the truth of healthy or at least intelligible human thought, emotion, and feeling.

Notoriously boring must be any oratorio, if the main idea is weakened by secondary ideas; if it wants to produce emotions without touching the depth of the soul, which is like reaping where it has not sowed; and if it gets lost in tirades that do not have any organic connection to the main plot.

Notoriously boring is and must be an oratorio, if, instead of persons and characters, it only portrays fading shadows of them, and introduces heroes, whom one would certainly not recognize as such except that much was made of their fame in reports constituted of recitative and if they did not stand out larger and more lordly in the story than is the case in such badly conceived oratorios, where the hero stumbles through the plot as if he was smitten with blindness.

Notoriously boring, finally, must be an oratorio, if it expects the audience to be touched emotionally in various ways without any clear motivation or reason.[14]

Keferstein brings up common points of criticism of *Paulus* in his list of warnings about oratorio writing. The first common complaint about Mendelssohn's *Paulus* is his use of chorales, which detracts from the drama and places the oratorio in the context of the lyric church oratorio:

It is questionable, if the insertion of the Christian chorale in the oratoric genre is helpful. In the old passions, from which the idea was taken, they are used for a reason, which is that passions are part of the worship service in which the congregation is to take part. The oratorio on the other hand has no part in actual worship; one could only label it church music, because it is performed in a church as pious entertainment or edification through music. . . . Whether the use of the chorale does not take away too much from the impact of the main characters, whether furthermore the chorale divides the attention of the listener, so that the listener can never follow the work as a unified whole, being pulled from too many sides, I cannot simply dismiss these questions.[15]

Keferstein's first warning is exactly about that danger. Second, Keferstein's warning about lacking focus by introducing secondary events is often pointed out in *Paulus* as weakness in Mendelssohn's lengthy heroic portrayal of Stephen: "We see that the overall conception of the work is too broad-based, especially in the beginning. These are actually two oratorios; the first being *Stephanus*, the other *Paulus*."[16] The third and most explicit stab at *Paulus* is found in Keferstein's warning against oratorios without real heroes, where "mit Blindheit geschlagen" entails a pun referring to the blinded Paul. Again, *Paulus* had been criticized for its weak second part, where, again, according to Fink, Paul's heroism is not exploited enough: "And yet, the second oratorio *Paulus* is approached too narrowly; Paul's softness and his fearful heart is more in the foreground than the apostolic power of his teaching. . . ."[17] Keferstein endorses Adolf Bernhard Marx's *Moses*, which Mendelssohn refused to premiere in Leipzig because of its poor quality, as the model for the modern oratorio. One might wonder if Keferstein's implied attacks on Mendelssohn's *Paulus* were motivated by the falling out between Marx and Mendelssohn over their failed attempts to write the respective librettos for each other for *Paulus* and *Moses*. The differences in opinion about the oratorio genre were nevertheless real.

Early Influences

The most profound early influence on Mendelssohn's understanding of musical genres was Carl Friedrich Zelter (1758-1832). He became Mendelssohn's teacher in 1819, when Mendelssohn was ten, the same year Zelter was given the task of establishing an Institute of Church Music.[18] Zelter's attempts to reform Prussian church music entailed the revival of the music of the old masters such as Palestrina and Bach. Mendelssohn joined Zelter's *Singakademie* in 1820 at the age of eleven. There he was exposed to the repertoire of the old masters. The thorough training in counterpoint, as well as the many sacred works written by the young Mendelssohn, attest to Mendelssohn's rich exposure to the music of the Renaissance and Baroque.[19]

Zelter's view of the oratorio was mostly shaped by the *empfindsam* church oratorio of the mid- to late-eighteenth century as well as Handel's oratorios—as can be seen in Zelter's only oratorio, *Auferstehung und Himmelfahrt* (1807), which is based on Ramler's continuation of his earlier libretto, *Der Tod Jesu*.[20] While Zelter regarded J. S. Bach's music very highly, it seems that for the oratorio Handel was the stronger model, as were composers such as Graun. As is well known, Zelter had serious doubts about a successful performance of Bach's *Matthäuspassion*.[21]

Johann Nepomuk Schelble (1789-1837), the music director of the Frankfurt *Cäcilienverein*, seems to have encouraged Mendelssohn in his plans to perform the *Matthäuspassion*, since the *Cäcilienverein* was planning its own performance.[22] Mendelssohn met Schelble for the first time in 1822, during a family trip to Switzerland. Mendelssohn made many subsequent visits to Frankfurt, during which their friendship was deepened. Mendelssohn dedicated several of his early sacred works to

Schelble.[23] Much like the *Singakademie* in Berlin, the *Cäcilienverein* was an oasis of the music of J. S. Bach, whose music was highly regarded for its depth of expression and meaningful content. In a letter to Zelter, Mendelssohn wrote about the *Cäcilienverein*:

> But on the other hand the *Cäcilienverein* is there, which alone is enough to make one glad to be in Frankfurt; these people sing with so much fire and are so in unison that it is a joy to behold. It meets once a week and has about two hundred members. But in addition Schelble gathers a smaller group of about thirty voices at his house on Friday evenings, where he has them sing at the piano and little by little works up his favorite pieces, which he doesn't dare present to the large association right away. There I heard a bunch of small Sunday pieces by Sebastian Bach, his *Magnificat*, the great Mass, and many other beautiful things as well. . . . I heard the motet *Gottes Zeit ist die allerbeste Zeit*, which we used to sing at your place on Fridays from time to time; the piece *Es ist der alte Bund* was quite divine with the big chorus and the beautiful, soft sopranos. One can scarcely believe what an effect a single person who wants to accomplish something can have on all the others.[24]

While Mendelssohn was also exposed to contemporaneous styles of music,[25] it was the church music of the past, especially the works of Bach, that he seemed to treasure the most in the early part of his life.

Other influences on Mendelssohn's approach to church music and the oratorio were Schleiermacher and Goethe. Schleiermacher, a member of the *Singakademie* in Berlin for twenty-five years, and Goethe both had a part in Zelter's attempts towards a reform of Protestant church music.[26] Mendelssohn visited Goethe on several occasions, and he attended lectures by Schleiermacher. Both encouraged the participation of the congregation in the worship service through singing;[27] Schleiermacher also emphasized the edifying function of sacred music.[28] These are important factors in Mendelssohn's understanding of church music, as will be shown later.

Performance Repertoire Up to *Paulus*

That Mendelssohn started his public conducting career with the performance of the *Matthäuspassion* on 11 March 1829 underlines his love for the music of Bach. During the same year, only one month later, Mendelssohn wrote to his mother, Lea, about a performance of Spohr's *Die letzten Dinge* by the *Singverein* in Hamburg:

The *Singverein* sounded quite good last night; they sang Spohr's *Die letzten Dinge* [. . .] The composition, however, is terrible; weariness and boredom are mistaken for edification by these people here, and they consider this music sacred; it is not sacred, but rather sinful play with trivialities. Jews are hanged for poisoning a well; but the music is surely worth as much as a well, I hope, which means that Spohr must die.[29]

It is important to note that Spohr's *Die letzten Dinge* was a church oratorio similar to Zelter's in its approach. While Mendelssohn was influenced by Zelter, he nevertheless clearly established his own approach different from that of Zelter. In fact, Zelter seemed to think Mendelssohn was too eager to follow Bach's ideals of church music writing rather than keeping up with the current styles and genres:

You seemed to be worried in your last letter that I, because of my love for one of the great masters, write so much church music in order to imitate him. However, that is surely not the case. . . . No one ought to keep me from enjoying and continuing with what the great masters left behind for me; nobody should have to start from the beginning once again, but rather, one has to continue according to one's own power, and not just create deadly repeats of what has already been done.[30]

During his employment at Düsseldorf from 1833 to 1835 Mendelssohn performed the following oratorios: Haydn's *Die Schöpfung* and *Die Jahreszeiten*, Handel's *Messiah*, *Israel in Egypt*, *Judas Maccabaeus*, *Samson*, *Alexanderfest*, *Semele*, and *Saul*, and Spohr's *Jessonda*.[31] He was also able to perform the Bach cantatas *Du Hirte Israel* (BWV 104) and *Gottes Zeit ist die allerbeste Zeit* (BWV 106) in Catholic church settings. Again, Mendelssohn's love for the older composers and his avoidance of contemporaneous composers can be seen in this repertoire.

A look at the programs of the Lower Rhine Music Festivals when Mendelssohn was the director shows the same type of repertoire: Handel oratorios, as much Bach as the committee and audience would allow, and not many choral works of later composers. Only for his first Lower Rhine Music Festival was Mendelssohn unable to select the program. The reaction by Abraham Mendelssohn to two cantatas by Ernst Wilhelm Wolff (1735-92) and Peter Winter (1754-1825) reflects surely his son's dislike for these pieces as well:

Last night was wonderful; the *Pastoral Symphony* went extremely
well, followed by a cantata by Wolff, which was deadly boring; then
Leonore was thrilling and striking. . . . Winter's *Macht der Töne*!
One of the two Woringen girls, who is very charming, summed up in
two words what can be said about Wolff's cantata and Winter's
Macht der Töne: Over *Macht der Töne* one might get angry; however, during the cantata one cannot help but fall asleep.[32]

Mendelssohn's Approach to Oratorio Writing

To gain an understanding of Mendelssohn's approach to the genre of
the oratorio, one first has to realize the composer's distinction between
liturgical music and music for edification. Mendelssohn wrote about
these two types of sacred music to Pastor Bauer, who had requested
that Mendelssohn write music for the church service:

> Actual church music—that is, music during the Evangelical Church
> service, which could be introduced properly while the service was be-
> ing celebrated—seems to me impossible; and that, not merely be-
> cause I cannot at all see into *which* part of the public worship this
> music can be introduced, but because I cannot discover that *any* such
> part exists. Perhaps you have something to say which may enlighten
> me on this subject. . . . But even without any reference to the Prussian
> Liturgy, which at once cuts off everything of the kind, and which
> will, probably, neither remain as it is nor go further, I do not see how
> it is to be managed that music in our church should form an integral
> part of public worship, and not become a mere concert, conducive
> more or less to piety. This was the case with Bach's "Passion;" it was
> sung at the church as an independent piece of music for edification.
> As for actual church music, or, if you like to call it so, music for pub-
> lic worship, I know none but the old Italian compositions for the Pa-
> pal chapel, where, however, the music is a mere accompaniment,
> subordinate to the sacred functions, co-operating with the wax can-
> dles and the incense, etc.[33]

At first glance this viewpoint seems close to that of Thibaut, one of the
foremost writers on church music at the time, with whom Mendelssohn
met:

> It is strange: this man does not know much about music, even his his-
> torical knowledge about it is quite limited, he just follows his in-
> stincts, I understand more about this than he—and yet I have learned
> much from him, for which I owe him thanks. For he has lit a spark in
> me for old Italian music, and his fire for it has warmed me. There is

such enthusiasm and glow in his talk; that is what I would call a
flowery language! We just bade each other farewell, and since I told
him many things about Seb. Bach and explained to him that the main
and most important things were still unknown to him, for in Sebastian
everything had come together, he said at our parting: "Farewell, and
may our friendship be established on Louis de Victoria and Sebastian
Bach. . . "[34]

While the two might have agreed on what liturgical music is, Mendelssohn also saw a place for Bach's music in the service—not as liturgical
music, but as music for edification. Mendelssohn, moreover, saw a
broader function in music for edification than just that of nonliturgical
music for the church. It was not confined to a church service, as the
performance of the *Matthäuspassion* attests: ". . . they sang with such
devotion, as if they were in church. The first two performances went
wonderfully, and it became clear once again that the audience is good;
they felt that this was not mere music and concert, this was about religion and church."[35]

   When Mendelssohn was asked in 1832 by Schelble to write an oratorio on Paul, he approached the oratorio—contrary to the modern, dramatic approach—as music for edification. His models, however, were
not the lyric, *empfindsam* oratorio but rather the large-scale choral
works of Bach and Handel. Mendelssohn realized that his idea of oratorio was different from the modern approach, as one can see in a letter
from his father, Abraham:

> The question, however, ought to be put in a different form,—not
> whether Handel would compose his oratorios now as he did a century
> since, but rather, whether he would compose any oratorios whatever;
> hardly—if they only could be written in the styles of those of the pre-
> sent day.
>   From my saying this to you may gather with what eager antici-
> pations and confidence I look forward to your oratorio, which will, I
> trust, solve the problem of combining ancient conceptions with mod-
> ern appliances; otherwise the result would be as great a failure as that
> of the painters of the nineteenth century, who only make themselves
> ridiculous by attempting to revive the religious elements of the fif-
> teenth, with its long arms and legs, and topsy-turvy perspective.[36]

   Felix Mendelssohn regarded the practician/composer rather than
the teacher/writer as the driving force for reform, which was never just
an attempt to recreate ideals from earlier times:

I am not acquainted with Herr W____, nor have I read his book; but
it is always to be deplored when any but genuine artists attempt to
purify and restore the public taste. On such a subject words are only
pernicious; deeds alone are efficient. For even if people do really feel
this antipathy towards the present, they cannot as yet give anything
better to replace it, and therefore they had best let it alone. Palestrina
effected a reformation during his life; he could not do so now any
more than Sebastian Bach or Luther. The men are yet to come who
will advance on the straight road; and who will lead others onwards
or back to the ancient and right path, which ought, in fact, to be
termed the onward path; but they will write no books on the subject.[37]

Both Gottfried Wilhelm Fink and Otto Jahn, in their discussions of
Paulus in 1837 and 1842, recognized Mendelssohn's intent of writing a
distinctly new type of oratorio in terms of nineteenth-century tradition,
based on the models of Bach and Handel.[38] Mendelssohn wanted to
write a work with spiritual substance in a time when the communal focus had shifted from the church to the concert hall. To Mendelssohn
and to many of his contemporaries, however, the concert hall was more
than a place of entertainment; it was a platform where profound ideas
and concepts were shared and where religious experiences were desired.

The fact that Mendelssohn wrote *Paulus* without a contemporaneous model in mind increases the importance of the evolution and revision process of his first oratorio tremendously. A careful analysis of the
evolution of *Paulus* will aid in gaining a better understanding of the
work and clarify Mendelssohn's approach to the oratorio and to sacred
music in general.

Notes

1. Johann Georg Sulzer, *Allgemeine Theorie der schönen Künste* (Leipzig: Weidmannsche Buchhandlung, 1793; reprint Hildesheim: Olms, 1967),
610-11: Ein mit Musik aufgeführtes geistliches, aber durchaus lyrisches und
kurzes Drama, zum gottesdienstlichen Gebrauch bey hohen Feyertagen. Die
Benennung des lyrischen Dramas zeiget an, daß hier seine sich allmählich
entwickelnde Handlung, mit Anschlägen, Intriguen und durch einander-
laufenden Unternehmungen statt habe, wie in dem für das Schauspiel verfertig-
ten Drama. Das Oratorium nimmt verschiedene Personen an, die von einem
erhabenen Gegenstand der Religion, dessen Feier begangen wird, stark gerührt
werden, und ihre Empfindungen darüber bald einzeln, bald vereinigt auf eine
sehr nachdrückliche Weise äußern. Die Absicht dieses Drama ist, die Herzen
der Zuhörer mit ähnlichen Empfindungen zu durchdringen.

Der Stoff des Oratorium ist also allemal eine sehr bekannte Sache, deren Andenken das Fest gewidmet ist. Folglich kann er durchaus lyrisch behandelt werden, weil hier weder Dialog noch Erzählungen, noch Nachrichten von dem was vorgeht, nöthig sind. Man weiß schon im voraus durch was für einen Gegenstand die Sänger in Empfindung gesetzt werden, und die Art, die besonderen Umstände derselben, unter denen der Gegenstand sich jedem zeiget. Dies alles kann aus der Art, wie sich die singenden Personen darüber auslassen, ohne eigentliche Erzählung hinlänglich bekannt werden. (All translations from sources in German are by the author.)

2. Howard E. Smither, *A History of the Oratorio*, vol. 3, *The Oratorio in the Classical Era* (Chapel Hill: University of North Carolina Press, 1987), 331-39.

3. G. A. Keferstein, "Das Oratorium," in *Allgemeine musikalische Zeitung* 50/51 (1843): col. 923:   die künstlerisch klare, vollgenügend lebenskräftige, dramatische Vergegenwärtigung einer gewichtvoll ansprechende Idee, in ihrer Bewegung vom thatsächlichen Werden zur Vollendung, durch das Mittel des reinen Musikwortes, ohne Intention auf theatralische Darstellung und ohne Nothwendigkeit derselben zur Erziehung des vollen Eindrucks.

4. Keferstein, col. 900: Ihr [Sulzer's Definition] zufolge soll das Oratorium ein Drama sein.—Ganz richtig! In älterer Zeit war es sogar, wie wir gesehen, ein wirklich theatralisches Drama. Wenn aber Sulzer "die allmählich sich entwickelnde Handlung," deren Darstellung ja auch, in einem grossen Bereiche, dem reinen Musikworte, ohne theatralische Hilfsmittel zugänglich ist; wenn er ferner alle Action und Reaction, alle Knotenschürzung und Lösung daraus verbannt wissen will, wo bleibt dann das Drama? Ist nicht ein solches Drama, wie Sulzer es will, am Ende so gut, wie ein Messer ohne Heft und Klinge? Bleibt dann dem Oratorium noch etwas anderes übrig, als das Gebiet nebelnder und schwebelnder Reflexion, welche, von Schattenpersonen getragen, wenn auch noch so lyrisch, ja gerade wenn recht hochlyrisch gehalten, kein Mensch auf längere Dauer zu ertragen vermag?

5. Keferstein, cols. 922-23: Rochlitz selbst dichtete ein Oratorium ("Die letzten Dinge"), welches, obgleich der Sulzer'schen Theorie völlig genügend und von Meister Spohr mit der herrlichsten lyrischen Musik ausgestattet, dennoch, wegen seines gänzlichen Mangels an dramatischer Klarheit und Lebenskraft, nicht zu so allgemeiner, dauernder Anerkennung gelangen konnte, wie sie die in vielen einzelnen Partieen wirklich himmlisch schöne Musik verdient hätte.

So ging es auch vielen anderen älteren und neueren Werken dieser Art. Fragt man aber, wie es gekommen, dass sich z.B. die Werke eines Händel und Haydn so lange in einer ungeschmälerten, ja steigenden Gunst beim Publicum halten konnten, so hat dies unstreitig darin seinen Grund, dass, wenn auch nicht die Texte dieser Meister, doch ihre Musik ein wahrhaft frisches, gesundes, dramatisches Leben athmet, welches sie oft da wo sie es bei ihren Dichtern nicht vorfanden, durch die Kraft ihres Genie's, wenigstens theilweise, zu erzeugen wussten.

Einzelne neuere Dichter und Componisten ahnten wohl, was dem Oratorium, dem so vielfach in einem todten Schlendrian versumpften, Noth war, allein aus Furcht vor dem Popanz einer von Haus aus todtgeborenen Theorie wagten sie nicht, es mit mutiger Consequenz zu ergreifen!—Die vorzüglichsten unter den Scheider'schen Oratorien brachten bereits zahlreiche erfreuliche Spuren warmer, dramatischer Bewegung, weshalb sie sich auch noch fortwährend in der Gunst des Publicums erhalten.

Näher und schärfer indess an die Idee des Oratorium, als wirkliches, reines Musikdrama gefasst, trat zuerst practisch Herr Professor Giesebrecht in Stettin (1835 und 1836), wiewohl im engeren Bereiche, in seinen beiden von Meister Löwe so geistreich componierten Vocaloratorien für Männerstimmen: "Die eherne Schlange' und "Die Apostel von Philippi" heran, während es Herrn Professor Marx vorbehalten blieb, durch seinen "Mose" das Oratorium aus der egyptischen Gefangenschaft falscher Theoremen vollends zu befreien und es in eine Richtung zu bringen, in welcher es sich nunmehr frei, reich und herrlich fortentwickeln kann.

6. For a discussion of Schneider's oratorios see Arnold Schering, *Geschichte des Oratoriums* (Leipzig: 1911; reprint, Hildesheim: 1968), 397-403.

7. Schering, 397.

8. Schering, 407.

9. See Georg Feder, "Verfall und Restauration," in *Geschichte der Evangelischen Kirchenmusik*, ed. Friedrich Blume (Kassel: Bärenreiter, 1965), 215-70.

10. Arnold Schering, *Geschichte des Oratoriums*, 397.

11. Cecelia Hopkins Porter, "The New Public and the Reordering of the Musical Establishment: The Lower Rhine Music Festivals, 1818-67," *19th-Century Music* 3/3 (March 1980): 211-24.

12. See table 1, Porter, 217.

13. Porter, 211.

14. G. A. Keferstein, "Das Oratorium," col. 924: Für alle drei Gattungen des Oratoriums gilt ein Hauptverbot: das der Langweiligkeit, wogegen sie, bei Todesstrafe der Vergessenheit, so interessant, belebt und erweckend, als nur möglich, sein müssen.

Notorisch langweilig aber wird und muss stets ein Oratorium sein, welches sich, ohne Verfolgung einer klaren Hauptidee, in vagen Räumen verliert, und in einer Lyrik umherschwebelt ohne festen Lebenskern des Handelns, Wirkens und Strebens aus der Wahrheit des gesunden oder doch wenigstens des begreiflichen Denkens, Fühlens und Empfindens heraus.

Notorisch langweilig muss das Oratorium sein, wenn das Hauptinteresse durch Nebeninteressen abschwächt; wenn es fromme Erregungen des Gemüthes, anstatt sie aus der Tiefe der Seele heraus zu erzeugen, ohne Weiteres machen und erzwingen, gleichsam ernten will, wo es nicht gesäet hat, und wenn es sich in langen und breiten Tiraden erschöpft, welche mit der Haupthandlung in keinem organischen Zusammenhang stehen.

Notorisch langweilig wird und muss ein Oratorium sein, wenn es anstatt Personen und Charactere, nur zerfliessende Schattenbilder aufstellt und Helden bringt, ohne sie in ihrer Tatkraft zu zeigen; Helden, welche man in solcher Zeichnung gar nicht anerkennen würde, wenn nicht von ihnen, etwa in recitativischen Berichterstattungen, viel Rühmens gemacht würde und wenn sie nicht überhaupt in der Geschichte viel grösser und herrlicher daständen, als sie in diesem oder jenen schief angelegten, und gleich, wie mit Blindheit geschlagen, zwischen grossen Personen und Ereignissen umhertappenden Oratorienwerke.

Notorisch langweilig muss endlich ein Oratorium sein, wenn es dem Anschauenden zumuthet, sich einmal über das andere, in die verschiedenartigsten Gemüthsbewegungen zu stürzen, ohne sie vorher gehörig motiviert zu haben.

15. See Gottfried Wilhelm Fink, "Paulus," *Allgemeine musikalische Zeitung* 39/31 (1837): cols. 519-20: Es fragt sich sogar noch sehr, ob die Einmischung der christlichen Choräle in's Oratorium demselben als eigenthümlichem Kunstwerke förderlich genannt werden kann. In den alten Passionen, woraus der Gedanke entlehnt ist, stehen sie mit Grund, denn die Passionswerke gehören zum kirchlichen Ritus, an welchem die Gemeinde Antheil nehmen soll. Dagegen nimmt das Oratorium keinen Theil an der eigentlichen Gottesverehrung; es ist nur kirchlich, weil es in der Kirche aufgeführt wird als eine für sich bestehende fromme Unterhaltung oder Erbauung durch Musik. . . . Ob aber der Antheil am Choral der Hauptperson nicht zu viel entzieht; ob er also die Interessen der Hörer nicht zu viel theilen hilf, so dass man endlich zu keinem haltbar sichern Einheitsgefühl kommen kann, weil der anziehenden Seiten zu viele sind, diese Fragen möcht ich nicht für überflüssig erklären.

16. Fink, col. 519: Wir sehen, die Anlage des Ganzen ist zu weit, namentlich was den Anfang betrifft. Es sind im Grunde 2 Oratorien; das erste Stephanus, das andere Paulus.

17. Fink, col. 519: Und doch ist das zweite Oratorium Paulus, um jenes willen wieder zu eng; des Paulus Weichheit des geänsteten Herzens tritt stärker hervor, als seine apostolische Grundgewalt thatreicher Lehrkraft.

18. Rudolf Werner, *Felix Mendelssohn Bartholdy als Kirchenmusiker* (Frankfurt: Rudolf Werner, 1930), 144.

19. See Larry Todd, *Mendelssohn's Musical Education: A Study and Edition of his Exercises in Composition: Oxford Bodleian ms. Margaret Deneke Mendelssohn C. 43* (Cambridge: Cambridge University Press, 1983).

20. For a discussion of Zelter's oratorio see Rudolf Werner, *Felix Mendelssohn Bartholdy als Kirchenmusiker* (Frankfurt: Rudolf Werner, 1930), 136-37.

21. Susanna Grossmann-Vendrey, *Felix Mendelssohn Bartholdy und die Musik der Vergangenheit* (Regensburg: Bosse, 1969), 29-30.

22. Carl Heinrich Müller, *Felix Mendelssohn: Frankfurt am Main und der Cäcilien-Verein* (Darmstadt: Scholle, 1925), 4.

23. Müller, 3-6: "Jube Domino" (1822), "Ave Maria" (1830, Op. 23 Nr. 2), cantata "Verleih uns Frieden" (1831), cantata "Ach Gott vom Himmel sieh darein" (1832).

24. *Felix Mendelssohn, A Life in Letters*, ed. Rudolf Elvers, trans. by Craig Tomlinson (New York: Fromm, 1986), 15 February 1832, 174-75.

25. See Susanna Grossmann-Vendrey, "Kindheit und Jugend," in *Felix Mendelssohn Bartholdy und die Musik der Vergangenheit* (Regensburg: Bosse, 1969), 13-28.

26. See W. Sattler, "Die Bedeutung der Singakademie zu Berlin für die liturgisch-musikalische Entwicklung Schleiermachers" *Zeitschrift für Musikwissenschaft*, 1 (1918-9), 165-76.

27. Sattler, 166.

28. Sattler, 170.

29. Felix Mendelssohn, *Felix Mendelssohn Bartholdy: Briefe*, ed. Rudolf Elvers (Franfurt: Fischer, 1984), 14 April 1829, 59-60: Der Singverein gestern war recht gut; er sang Spohrs letzte Dinge [. . .] Aber die Komposition ist ganz schändlich, Mattigkeit und Langeweile halten die Leute für Erbauung, und finden die Musik heilig, sie ist aber unheilig, und ein sündliches Spiel mit Kleinigkeiten. Man hängt die Juden wenn sie einen Brunnen vergiften; aber die Musik ist ebensoviel werth, hoffe ich als ein Brunnen, und somit muß Spohr sterben.

30. Felix Mendelssohn in a letter to Zelter, 18 December 1830; quoted in Annemarie Clostermann, *Mendelssohn Bartholdys kirchenmusikalisches Schaffen* (Mainz: Schott, 1989), 31-32: Sie schienen mir in Ihrem vorigen Brief zu fürchten, ich möchte, durch Vorliebe für irgendeinen der großen Meister geleitet, mich viel an Kirchenmusik machen, um mich einer Nachahmung hinzugeben. Das ist aber wohl bestimmt nicht der Fall. (. . .) Freilich kann mir niemand verwehren, mich dessen zu erfreuen und an dem weiter zu arbeiten, was mir die großen Meister hinterlassen haben, denn von vorne soll wohl nicht jeder wieder anfangen aber es soll auch ein Weiterarbeiten nach Kräften sein, nicht ein totes Wiederholen des schon Vorhandenen.

31. Susanna Grossmann-Vendrey, *Felix MendelssohnBartholdy und die Musik der Vergangenheit*. Regensburg 1969. (Studien zur Musikgeschichte des 19. Jahrhunderts, vol. 17), 63-64.

32. Abraham Mendelssohn in a letter; quoted in Susanna Grossmann-Vendrey, *Felix Mendelssohn Bartholdy und die Musik der Vergangenheit*, 73: Gestern abend war es schön; die Symphonie Pastorale ging ganz vortrefflich, darauf eine Cantate von Wolff tödtlich langweilig; dann Leonore allgemain hinreissend und einschlagend. . . . Winters Macht der Töne! Eine der beiden Woringen, ein ganz charmantes Mädchen, hat in zwei Worten über Wolffs Cantate und Winters Macht der Töne alles erschöpft, was sich darüber sagen läßt: Über die Macht der Töne kann man sich noch ärgern, aber bei der Cantate muß man einschlafen.

33. Felix Mendelssohn, *Letters from 1833 to 1847*, ed. Paul and Carl Mendelssohn-Bartholdy; trans. by Lady Wallace (London: Longman, Green and Co., 1890), 12 January 1835, 63-64.

34. Felix Mendelssohn in a letter to Lea Mendelssohn, dated 20 September 1827; quoted in Susanna Grossmann-Vendrey, *Felix Mendelssohn Bartholdy und die Musik der Vergangenheit*, 24: Es ist sonderbar: der Mann weiß wenig

von Musik, selbst seine historischen Kenntnisse darin sind ziemlich beschränkt, er handelt meist nach bloßem Instinkt, ich verstehe mehr davon als er—und doch habe ich unendlich viel von ihm gelernt, bin ihm gar vielen Dank schuldig. Denn er hat mir ein Licht für die altitalienische Musik aufgehen lassen und an seinem Feuersturm hat er mich erwärmt. Das ist eine Begeisterung und eine Glut, mit der er redet, das nenne ich eine blumige Sprache! Ich komme eben vom Abschiede her, und da ich ihm manches vom Seb. Bach erzählte und ihm gesagt hatte, das Haupt und das Wichtigste sei ihm unbekannt, denn im Sebastian, da sei alles zusammen, so sprach er zum Abschiede: "Leben sie wohl, und unsere Freundschaft wollen wir an den Louis de Vittoria und den Sebastian Bach anknüpfen . . ."

35. Felix Mendelssohn in a letter to Franz Hauser, dated 16 April 1830; quoted in Carl Dahlhaus, "Mendelssohn und die musikalische Gattungstradition," in *Das Problem Mendelssohn* (Regensburg: Bosse, 1974), 58: . . . sie sangen mit einer Andacht, als ob sie in der Kirche wären. So gingen denn auch die beiden ersten Aufführungen ganz herrlich und es zeigte sich wieder, daß das Publicum immer gut ist, sie fühlten, daß hier nicht Musik und Concert, sondern Religion und Kirche sei.

36. Abraham Mendelssohn, *Letters from 1833 to 1847*, 10 March 1835, 72.

37. Abraham Mendelssohn, *Letters from 1833 to 1847*, 4 March 1833, 2.

38. Gottfried Wilhelm Fink, "Paulus," *Allgemeine musikalische Zeitung* 39/31-32 (1837): cols. 497-506, 513-30. Otto Jahn, Über Felix Mendelssohn Bartholdy's Oratorium Paulus, Kiel: 1842; also in Allgemeine musikalische Zeitung 50 (1848): cols. 113-22, 137-43, and in Gesammelte Aufsätze über Musik. Leipzig: Breitkopf und Härtel, 1866.

Chapter 2

The Sources: Description and Chronology

Libretto Sources

On 20 December 1831 Mendelssohn mentioned for the first time the idea of writing an oratorio on the New Testament character Paul.[1] Mendelssohn spent the next two and a half years working on the libretto for this project. It was not until the spring of 1834 that Mendelssohn started composing the work.[2] Jeffrey Sposato has transcribed and discusses all the libretto sources for *Paulus* in his dissertation.[3] Table 2.1 lists the precompositional libretto sources for *Paulus*, all of which are found in the Margaret Deneke Mendelssohn collection in the Bodleian Library in Oxford. There are two further libretto sources for the first performance: *MDM d. 30, no. 216b, 217*, a draft by Mendelssohn and another unidentified hand; and a printed program of the premiere on 22 May 1836.

Musical Sources

Autographs

The compositional process of *Paulus* was long and tedious, lasting from spring 1834 until winter of 1836-37. There are many different musical sources for *Paulus*—autographs, manuscript copies, and a

Table 2.1. The Precompositional Libretto Sources of *Paulus*

MDM c. 42, fol. 2-3—22 December 1832, draft by Mendelssohn, sent to Schubring

MDM d. 30, no. 214, fol. 407-408—23 January 1833, draft by Schubring, sent
to Mendelssohn

MDM d. 53, no. 87 (IIIa) and d. 30, no. 211, fols. 409-410 supplement (IIIb)—
undated draft by Fürst

MDM d. 53, no. 88—15 March 1833, draft by Marx

MDM d. 30, no. 211—5 October 1833, draft by Mendelssohn, sent to Schubring

MDM c. 27, p. 28r-30v—undated draft by Mendelssohn

MDM c. 27, p. 31r-32r—undated draft by Mendelssohn

Korrekturabzug. Two important sources are in the Staatsbibliothek zu
Berlin—Preussischer Kulturbesitz: *Mus. ms. autogr. Mendelssohn 19*
(hereafter abbreviated as MN19) contains sketches and drafts of various
movements of *Paulus. Mus. ms. autogr. Mendelssohn 28* (MN28) contains, besides other compositions, several rejected movements of *Paulus.* Of the autographs, the three most complete sources are *Mus. ms.
autogr. Mendelssohn 53* (MN53), *Mus. ms. autogr. Mendelssohn 54*
(MN54), and *Mus. ms. autogr. Mendelssohn 55* (MN55). All three volumes are presently held in the Jagiellonian Library in Kraków, Poland.
MN53 contains a full score of the first part of the oratorio; MN54, a full
score of the second part; and MN55, a piano-vocal score of both parts
of the oratorio. The remaining autograph sources are only single pages
of earlier versions of *Paulus.* No autograph fair copy is extant. All of
these sources differ from the first published (Simrock) version.

MN53 and MN54

MN53 and MN54 are bound in the typical green covers of Mendelssohn's numbered manuscript volumes, collected by the composer and
bound in 1845.[4] Both autographs are made up of bifolios and single
leaves of three different paper types. These scores do not represent just
one stage of the compositional process; rather, Mendelssohn drew from

several earlier autographs to arrive at these versions. Both versions were dated close to the premiere of *Paulus* (22 May 1836); MN53 is dated 8 April 1836, MN54 is dated 18 April 1836. Table 2.2 gives a description of the paper types.

Table 2.2. Description of Paper Types of MN53 and MN54

Paper A:
> Size of leaf: 305 mm X 217 mm
> Staves: 16 – 254 mm X 193 mm
> Quality: very thin; cut, straight edges on all four   sides; the most accurately made paper of the three

Paper B:
> Size of leaf: 328 mm (±3) X 247 mm (±3)
> Staves: 16 – 270 mm X 218 mm
> Quality: thick and heavy; cut, straight edges on all four sides

Paper C:
> Size of leaf:
> > cut on one side (top or bottom), slit on the other sides:
> > > 318 mm (±3) X 236 mm (±5)
> > cut on both sides: 315 mm (±3) X 236 mm (±5)
> Staves: 12 – 245 mm X 185 mm
> Quality: very thick and heavy; most of the time only one side is cut, the other is slit
> Dealer's mark: "Bonn bei N. Simrock" printed vertically across the inside of each bifolio
> Watermark: "C.F." at bottom of bifolio[5]

The structure of MN53 is more complex than that of MN54. Paper changes are more frequent, and there are more paste-overs and crossed-out pages. There are seven different page/leaf/bifolio numberings, of which only two are continuous throughout the autograph. The first one is a librarian's numbering of the manuscript, taking paste-overs into account. The second numbering is in Mendelssohn's hand; it consecutively numbers the recto side of each leaf, without taking paste-overs into account. The next two page numberings have to be seen together, since the fourth page numbering starts approximately where the third numbering leaves off. Even though the third numbering continues sporadically for another eight pages, it continues in black pencil, while it was in red pencil before. At number 50 the fourth numbering goes back

to red pencil in yet another hand, which continues for the remainder of
the manuscript. The most plausible explanation for the fourth and fifth
numberings is suggested by a letter from Mendelssohn, written on 30
March 1836, to Ferdinand von Woringen, one of the main organizers of
the Lower Rhine Music Festival: "Of my full score of the oratorio I will
send a copy to Düsseldorf, and I am asking you to take charge of the
copying of the instrumental and solo parts. The first part will be in your
hands during the first half of the next month, the second part in the last
half of next month."[6] It seems likely that several copyists could have
numbered the score according to how far each was to copy it. Unac-
counted for, however, is the omission of two pages in the fourth numbering (between numbers 9 and 10). The only explanation might be that
the copyist skipped those two pages inadvertently. The fact that the thin
A paper is used there speaks for this explanation. The fifth column contains three different local numberings in Mendelssohn's hand, representing the earliest numberings, because these are the only numbers
that appear to date from before the consolidation of different scores.
See chapter 4 for a closer look at these earlier page numberings.

MN54 is a much cleaner and less revised manuscript than MN53.
MN54 is almost completely made up of bifolios. Only once was Mendelssohn not able to use a bifolio, as he had to insert a single leaf
(pages 13 and 14).

Four different page numberings appear in MN54, not one of which
is continuous. The first two numberings together, however, make a continuous numbering. The second numbering does not start until page 31
of the score, which is where the first numbering shows an insertion of a
bifolio numbered 30a, 30b, 30c, and 30d. The numbers on the inserted
bifolio are the only numberings in Mendelssohn's hand. He apparently
numbered them so that the copyist could find the right place to insert
them. The numbers surrounding the insertion are continuous. The second numbering, starting with the inserted bifolio, continues the first
numbering. Presumably the second numbering was added by the librarian, who saw no need to write a new set of numberings into the score
until the existing numbering was incorrect. The fact that only every
recto side is marked with a number, which is a common librarian's
numbering system, underlines this assumption.

The third numbering starts with number 1, where the second numbering leaves off (50), counting every bifolio rather than every page or
leaf. The reason for this abrupt numbering change is explained in a letter by Mendelssohn to the committee of the Lower Rhine Music Festival on 16 April 1836:

> I send you the full score of my oratorio (the first part and numbers 26-31 of the second part). The rest of the second part will follow in a few days. I assume that the parts can be copied better and more correctly there than they would be here, since I had to check this copy note by note, and I am still afraid that some mistakes may have sneaked in.[7]

The second numbering stops with the last page of no. 31, confirming that MN54 was the full score Mendelssohn used immediately before the premiere.[8] The letter also shows, however, that Mendelssohn did not send MN54 to Düsseldorf; rather, he sent a copy of the score, which is no longer extant. The third numbering shows some inconsistencies, because bifolios 6 and 8 do not show their numbering. The fourth numbering counts every leaf of the manuscript, displaying its numbering only on every tenth leaf. This numbering must have been entered very recently, since it does not appear on the microfilm copy.

MN55

Presumably, MN55 was not been bound at the same time as MN53 and MN54, because it has brown covers. On the spine of the binding it reads "Mendelssohn, Paulus," "Clavierauszug," and "Autograph." Since there is no inscription indicating that MN54 and MN55 are autographs, it seems plausible that MN55 was not originally bound as part of Mendelssohn's collection of manuscripts. Inside the front cover of the manuscript is a letter, dated 5 January 1837, from Mendelssohn to Conrad Schleinitz, to whom Mendelssohn sent MN55:

> Here is the piano reduction of *Paulus*, which has been long delayed but which you may nevertheless gladly receive from me, and under which you have to put music. Since I usually forget what I was going to say to you, I have to write you that for the last three days I was going to ask you to lend me the soprano aria "Der du die Menschen lässest sterben" from my written piano reduction for a while, since my sister would like to have it in Berlin, and since I do not have it. You will get it back right after her performance there, and you would do me a big favor, if you have it brought to me by the messenger. Your Felix Mendelssohn.[9]

Mendelssohn must have sent Schleinitz MN55 as a gift, since it contains an earlier, obsolete version of the oratorio. The requested aria was one that was cut after the first performance. Even though it was still included in MN55, there must have been a revised version that Mendelssohn wanted.

As is the case with the full score of *Paulus* contained in MN53 and MN54, MN55 is also a compilation made up of earlier drafts together with new material, which can be seen through the use of different paper types. MN55, however, only shows two different types of paper, type B and type C.

MN55 contains both parts of the oratorio in piano-vocal score. The second part, however, shows heavier revision than the first part. While the first part of the oratorio uses only complete bifolios, the second part frequently uses single leaves. MN55 shows eight page numberings, but only one of them is continuous. It is in Mendelssohn's hand and counts every leaf rather than every page, which is how Mendelssohn typically numbered his manuscripts. Four numberings together also number the whole manuscript. The first two numberings split the first part of the oratorio evenly, numbering every bifolio. The third numbering starts at the beginning of part 2, counting every leaf; at first a number appears on every page (9), then on every recto side. This numbering then stops with number 20, and the fourth numbering starts with number 21. The fourth numbering, however, counts only every leaf rather than every page. Perhaps the writer of the fourth numbering only saw the last number of the third numbering and assumed that every leaf was counted. These four numberings might have been used to divide the manuscript for copying. The presence of copyists' markings throughout MN55 clearly shows that this manuscript was copied at some point. The other numberings are local.

MN28

Only a part of MN28 contains material from *Paulus*. All of the movements of *Paulus* in MN28 were rejected in the later, complete drafts. These rejected movements were written on paper of types A and C. The only set of page numberings found in these pages of MN28 is that of the librarian, who counted every page, entering numbers on the recto side of each leaf. Even the pages of numbered movements, some of which presumably were part of a complete draft, do not show any other page numberings. It appears that Mendelssohn did not routinely number drafts continuously until the compilation drafts of MN53 and MN54.

MN19

MN19 contains a collection of preliminary drafts and sketches in various stages, as well as some discarded material from fair copies of completed works. Only pages 1 and 4-14 contain material from *Paulus*. Douglass Seaton gives a detailed account of the structure and content of these pages of MN19 in his dissertation.[10]

Other Autographs

Table 2.3 shows the other autographs of parts of movements of *Paulus*.

Table 2.3. Other Autographs of *Paulus*

Bibliothèque du Conservatoire Royal de Musique Brussels (B-Bc)   *Ms. 1092*—leaf of an earlier version of "Steiniget ihn" (No. 9).
Hessische Landes- und Hochschulbibliothek Darmstadt (D-DS)   *Mus. ms. 1445b*—one leaf containing "Doch der Herr er leitet der Irrenden recht," op. 112 Nr. 1, originally intended for *Paulus*.
Stanford University Library, Stanford, California (US-STu)   One page of musical memento written by Mendelssohn of the opening theme of "So sind wir denn nun Botschafter."

The first of these three autographs is a single leaf with music in full score from the chorus "Steiniget ihn" from part 1 of the oratorio. At the bottom of the verso side Felix Mendelssohn's brother Paul wrote, "This leaf is taken from a handwritten, musical sketchbook of my brother Felix. Berlin, 13 February. Paul Mendelssohn Bartholdy."[11] *Ms. 1092* does not seem to be taken from the autograph full score of part 1, MN53, since MN53 uses paper of type B for that chorus (pp. 80-86), while *Ms. 1092* was written on type A paper.

The second of these single-leaf autographs shows a piano-vocal score of the rejected aria No. 16 "Doch der Herr er leitet die Irrenden recht." It is written on type B paper. *Mus. Ms. 1445b* is part of a collection of manuscripts compiled by the singer Franz Hauser (1794-1810).

The third of these autographs is less interesting for this study, because it is only a musical memento that Mendelssohn wrote down from memory. It is dated 22 May 1838.

Manuscript Copies

PS-NYPL

Drexel Collection 4779 (New York Public Library), a hand copy of a piano-vocal score (hereafter abbreviated as PS-NYPL), is not identical with any of the other sources. It is fairly close, however, to MN55. The first page shows the following remark, "This piano reduction follows the first version of *Paulus*, performed in Düsseldorf in the year 1836. It is the only existing copy of this kind. . . . Julius Rietz."[12] PS-NYPL is written on paper of type C. There is one continuous set of page numberings from the opening chorus to the end; the overture is numbered separately in the same hand. Every page is numbered, and a number appears on the recto side of each leaf. Starting at page 49, there appears a second numbering; pages 49 through 51 are also numbered 18 through 20.

Other Manuscript Copies

There are two manuscript copies of piano-vocal scores of single arias that were rejected (see Table 2.4).

Table 2.4. Other Manuscript Copies

Staatsbibliothek zu Berlin—Preussischer Kulturbesitz (D-B)
> *Mus. ms. autogr. Mendelssohn 20*, pp. 55-57—manuscript copy by Marie Mendelssohn of a piano-vocal score of No. 16, "Doch der Herr er leitet die Irrenden recht."

Bodleian Library, Oxford (GB-OB)
> *MDM c. 23, fols. 24-27*—manuscript copy in unidentified hand of [No. 11] "Der du die Menschen lässest sterben"

Both arias also appear as autographs. The autograph of "Doch der Herr er leitet die Irrenden recht" became part of Franz Hauser's manuscript collection; "Der du die Menschen lässest sterben" is found in both MN53 and MN54. These two arias were posthumously published in 1868 as op. 112, nos. 1 and 2.

Korrekturabzug

The Simrock archives, owned by the music publisher Anton Benjamin in Hamburg, include the *Korrekturabzug* (plate number 3320) of *Paulus*, containing pages 1-254 of the first edition of the full score with Mendelssohn's corrections. The composer corrected pitches and added missing metronome markings and organ entrances. All of Mendelssohn's changes were transferred into the engraving for the first edition.

Notes

1. Felix Mendelssohn, *Felix Mendelssohn-Bartholdys Briefwechsel mit Legationsrat Karl Klingemann in London*, ed. Karl Klingemann Jr. (Essen: G.D. Baedeker, 1909), 90: Meinen lieben Bruder Paul grüsse ein paarmal und sage, er möge nicht brummen über mein langes Pausieren; ich schreibe ihm in den nächsten Tagen. Sag' ihm, dass ich Auftrag auf ein Oratorium habe, das den Titel seines Namensvetters, des Apostels, führen wird, und in dem eine Predigt vorkommen soll.

2. Mendelssohn, 25 April 1834, 130: Mein Oratorium ist angefangen und ich habe sonst viel zu tun und zu arbeiten, bin also wohl.

3. Jeffrey Sposato, "Mendelssohn's Theological Evolution: A Study of Textual Choice and Change in the Composer's Sacred Works," Ph.D. diss., Brandeis University, 1999.

4. See Douglass Seaton, "A Study of a Collection of Mendelssohn's Sketches and Other Autograph Material: Deutsche Staatsbibliothek Berlin MUS. Ms. Autogr. Mendelssohn 19," Ph.D. diss., Columbia University, 1977, 1-2, 17.

5. This watermark appears only once in all the manuscripts of *Paulus*, in MN54, 47 (see appendix, p. 292).

6. Felix Mendelssohn, Leipzig, to Ferdinand von Woringen, Düsseldorf, ALS, 30 March 1836, Heinrich-Heine-Institut Düsseldorf, Musikvereinsdepos. letter 10: Von meiner Partitur des Oratoriums werde ich eine Abschrift nach Düsseldorf schicken, und dich bitten, das Ausschreiben der Instrumental- und Solostimmen dort zu besorgen. Der erste Theil wird in der ersten Hälfte, und der zweite in der letzten Hälfte des nächsten Monat's in Deine Hände gelangen.

7. Felix Mendelssohn, Leipzig, to the Committee of the Lower Rhine Music Festival, Düsseldorf, ALS, 16 April 1836, Heinrich-Heine-Institut Düsseldorf, Musikvereinsdepos. letter 13: . . . übersende ich hierbei die Partitur meines Oratoriums (den ersten Theil und vom zweiten die Nummern 26-31 incl.). Der Rest des zweiten Theiles wird in wenigen Tagen nachfolgen. Ich setze voraus, daß die Stimmen dort besser und correcter ausgeschrieben werden können, als es hier geschehen würde, da ich sogar diese Abschrift Note für Note durchsehen mußte, und dennoch fürchte, daß sich Fehler eingeschlichen haben werden.

8. Ralf Wehner already pointed this out in his unpublished paper, "Ein anderer 'Paulus?': Bemerkungen zu einer unbekannten Fassung des Mendelssohnschen Oratoriums" (Leipzig), 5-6.

9. Felix Mendelssohn, *Mus. ms. autogr. Mendelssohn 55*, letter inside the front cover: Hiebei der Klavierauszug meines Paulus, der lang verspätet ist aber den sie auch jetzt noch freundlich von mir annehmen, u. unter ihm Noten legen müssen. Und da ich gewöhnlich vergesse, was ich ihnen sagen wollte, so muß ich schreiben daß ich Sie schon seit 3 Tagen bitten wollte mir aus meinem geschriebenen Clavier-Auszug die Sopran Arie "Der du die Menschen lässest sterben" auf einige Zeit zu leihen, da meine Schwester in Berlin sie gerne haben will, u. ich sie nicht besitze. Sie erhalten sie gewiß gleich nach ihrer dortigen Aufführung wieder, u. thäten mir einen Gefallen, wenn sie mir sie durch den Unterbringer zuschickten. Ihr Felix Mendelssohn

10. Douglass Seaton, "A Study of a Collection of Mendelssohn's Sketches and Other Autograph Material," 3.

11. Paul Mendelssohn, *MS 1092*, Biblioteque du Conservatoire Royal de Musique Brussels: Dieses Blatt ist einem handschriftlichen, musikalischen Skizzenbuch meines Bruders Felix entnommen. Berlin 13. Februar 1854. Paul Mendelssohn Bartholdy.

12. Dieser Klavierauszug ist nach der ersten Bearbeitung des Paulus, im Jahre 1836, in Düsseldorf aufgeführt. Es ist das einzige in dieser Art existierende Exemplar. . . . Julius Rietz.

Chapter 3

The Phases of the
Compositional Process of *Paulus*

Overview

The compositional process of *Paulus* shows five distinct phases. These five phases are delineated by chronology as well as by the autographs and manuscripts. A general timetable of the composition of *Paulus* is easily established through Mendelssohn's correspondence. Table 3.1 shows the basic chronology of *Paulus*.

The first four phases occurred before the premiere of *Paulus* on 22 May 1836 at the 18th Lower Rhine Music Festival in Düsseldorf. The last phase represents revisions made by the composer after the premiere but before the publication of *Paulus*. The piano-vocal score was published in November 1836; the full score, in February 1837.

The autographs and manuscripts represent material from the first four phases of the compositional process. Table 3.2 shows how the manuscript material represents the first four compositional phases.

There are no autographs or manuscripts extant that represent phase 5. Since most autographs and manuscript copies represent several compositional phases, a breakdown of the individual sources is necessary in order to gain a better understanding of the compositional process as shown in the autographs. Because Mendelssohn completed movements first in full score, and since only movements in full score represent

every phase, a look at all the sources containing movements in full
score seems the most helpful. Table 3.3 shows a breakdown of MN53,
MN54, and MN28. Movements found in MN28 are italicized; rejected
movements are marked with an asterisk [*].

Table 3.1. The Chronology of *Paulus*

Phase 1: April-August 1834, Düsseldorf; composition of most of part 1 of
          Paulus

Phase 2: November 1834-May 1835, Düsseldorf; finishing part 1, composition
          of part 2 of *Paulus*

Phase 3: August-December 1835, Leipzig; revision of the previous material
          and creation of a complete draft of *Paulus*

Phase 4: January-April 1836, Leipzig; revision the previous material and crea-
          tion of the first performance version

Phase 5: June-August 1836, Frankfurt; revision of the first performance ver-
          sion and creation of the published, final version

Table 3.2. Phases 1-4 in Autographs and Manuscripts

Phase 1	Phase 2	Phase 3	Phase 4
MN19	MN19	MN19	
MN28	MN28	MN28	
MN53		MN53	MN53
	MN54	MN54	MN54
		MN55	MN55
Ms. 1092			
			PS-NYPL
			Mus. Ms. 1445b

Table 3.3. Phases in MN53, MN54, and MN28

Phase 1 April-August 1834	Phase 2 August-November 1835	Phase 3 December 1835-April 1836
		1. Ouverture
	2. Herr, der du bist	
	3. Die Menge der Gläubigen	
	*2. Ach bleib' mit deiner Gnade	
	*3. Die Menge der Gläubigen	
	4. [2.] Allein Gott in der Höh'	
	5. Stephanus aber	
	*4. Die Menge der Gläubigen	
	[5.] Wir haben ihn gehört Und bewegten das Volk	
	6.[4., 5.] Dieser Mensch	
7. [5.] Und sie sahen auf ihn Weg, weg mit dem		
		[7.] Siehe, ich sehe
		8. [6.] Jerusalem
		9. [7., 8.] Sie aber stürmten Steiniget ihn
	10. Und sie steinigten ihn Dir, Herr, will ich	
	11. Der du die Menschen [90]	11. Der du die Menschen [90-93]
		12. Es bestellten aber
13. [9] Siehe, wir preisen		
14. Und die Zeugen hatten		
	*13. Herr Gott, deß die Rache	14. Vertilge sie
		15. Saulus aber zerstörte
		16. Doch der Herr vergißt
	17. Und als er auf dem [121-22]	17. Und als er auf dem [117-20]
18. [15.] Mache dich auf [123-24]	18. [15.] Mache dich auf [123-24]	
19. [16.] Wachet auf		
	20. [17.] Die Männer aber	
	21. [18.] Gott, sei mir gnädig	
	22. [19.] Es war aber ein Jünger	
	23. [20.] Ich danke dir, Herr Der Herr wird die Tränen	
	24. [21.] Und Ananias ging	
*Die unter euch Gott [253-54]		
*Mit unsrer Macht		
25. [22.] O welch eine Tiefe		

Continued on next page

(Table 3.3—*Continued*)

Phase 1 April-August 1834	Phase 2 August-November 1835	Phase 3 December 1835-April 1836
26. Der Erdkreis ist nun		26. Der Erdkreis ist nun
		27. Und Paulus kam
	*28 Die unter euch Gott	
	28. So sind wir nun	
	29. Wie lieblich sind	
	30. Und wie sie ausgesandt	
	Da aber die Juden das Volk	
	So spricht der Herr	
	31. Und sie stellten Paulus nach	
	Ist das nicht	
	O Jesu Christe	
		32. Da sprach Paulus
		33. Da das aber die Heiden
		Die Götter sind
*32. Danket den Göttern		
	34. Und nannten Barnabas	
	35. Seyd uns gnädig	
*Lobt Ihn mit Pfeifen		
*Danket dem Gott		
*Danket dem Herrn		
	36. Da das die Apostel	
	37. Wisset ihr nicht	
38. Aber unser Gott		
39. Da ward das Volk erreget		
40. Hier ist des Herren		40. Hier ist des Herren
		41. Und sie alle verfolgten
		Sey getreu bis in den Tod
*Gelobet sei Gott der Vater		
*Schnell aber ward		
*O treuer Heiland		
		42. Erhebe dich
*Paulus sandte hin		43. Paulus sandte hin
*Schone doch deiner selbst	[43.] Schone doch deiner selbst	Schone doch deiner selbst
	Was machet ihe	
	Des Herrn Wille geschehe	
	Und als er das gesagt	
	44. Sehet, welch eine Liebe	
45. Und wenn er schon	45. Und wenn er schon	
		46. Nicht aber ihm allein

Phase 1

After he worked on the libretto for over two years, Mendelssohn started composing *Paulus* in the spring of 1834. On 28 March 1834 Mendelssohn wrote to his father, *"Paulus* has also made quite good progress and I intend to start writing before Pentecost."[1] A few weeks later, on 25 April, Mendelssohn reported to Klingemann that he had started composing the oratorio.[2] Another week later, on 2 May, Mendelssohn reported that he had written two movements of the oratorio and hoped to finish at least the first part of the oratorio by fall.[3] During the next few weeks Mendelssohn completely dedicated himself to the composition of the oratorio, even canceling a trip to England: "Warm days, and so delightfully long, and I have already begun my Oratorio, which is the reason I cannot go to the Westminster Abbey Festival, but must keep to my work."[4] In a letter on 6 June to his mother, Mendelssohn laid out his plans concerning *Paulus*: "I am working quite a lot now, and I feel great. I have finished a few more choruses of *Paulus* since then; if, however, Schelble will be able to perform *Paulus* already next winter, as he would like to, is questionable, but I have not answered him yet, and it will depend on the success of my work in the next few weeks."[5]

Even though Mendelssohn had worked on the libretto for over two years, he only used his libretto drafts as starting points, as he explained to Fürst on 20 July 1834:

> When I am composing, I usually look at the scriptural passages myself, and thus you will find that much is simpler, shorter, and more compressed than in your text; whereas at that time I could not get words enough, and was constantly longing for more. Since I have set to work, however, I feel very differently, and I can now make a selection. The first part will probably be finished next month, and the whole, I think, by January.[6]

The first compositional phase of *Paulus* came to an end with the beginning of the concert and theater season in Düsseldorf. Mendelssohn almost reached his goal of composing the first part of the oratorio, finishing part 1 at the beginning of the second phase in November; he reported to Klingemann on 16 December 1834 that he was already working on part 2 of the oratorio.[7]

Phase 2

After a two-month break Mendelssohn was eager to get back to work on *Paulus* in November. Obviously he had not been able to finish the oratorio in time for a performance by Schelble's *Cäcilienverein* in Frankfurt. Even the next possible performance date at the Lower Rhine Music Festival did not give Mendelssohn enough time to finish the oratorio:

> Only since then [Düsseldorf duties] have I been able get to work, but with what joy! . . . It is too bad that I just now receive an inquiry about a performance of my oratorio at Pentecost in Cologne, and that I have to decline because of the lost time; if I could have worked those two months, I would have been able to perform it. . . .[8]

All winter Mendelssohn worked almost exclusively on *Paulus*, as he wrote to Klingemann on 16 February 1835:

> I have never lived so completely alone, at least intellectually or musically, as I have this winter. I see one 15th after the next approaching, and realize that something lies in between them only because of the growing number of bifolios of my oratorio and the dwindling blank staff paper from Berlin.[9]

During this intense second phase, Mendelssohn used "staff paper from Berlin." Mendelssohn used the same type of paper for phases 1 and 2; it will be shown later that it was paper of type A. The composer had hoped to finish the oratorio in March or April in order to take a trip to England. As in the year before, however, Mendelssohn canceled the trip because of his desire to finish the oratorio:

> In the beginning I tried to make the trip in May, but it finally did not work out and I should have written it to you after two weeks and postponed it from one day to the next. First the oratorio expanded, and will hardly be finished before the middle of May. . . . It also so happens that the Hensels will probably attend the Music Festival and then stay a few days in Düsseldorf. There is much to do anyway for the Festival; in short, in order to finish the oratorio and not to neglect my directorship here, I have to stay here through the middle of June in any case. At the same time, Schelble wrote me from Frankfurt, that he hopes to perform *Paulus* for the first time in October or November; therefore after the Music Festival I intend to take the full score to Frankfurt to consult with him and then (in July) travel for several weeks to Switzerland or England, or to my parents.[10]

Mendelssohn spent the rest of the spring working intensely on the oratorio until the music festival on 8-9 June in Cologne: "I live very quietly and alone, often speak no more to a human than to my horse. And so the oratorio is making good progress, and as soon as it is finished the symphonies are next."[11] He was able to finish the second part of the oratorio before the music festival, to which his parents also came. After they had spent time together in Düsseldorf, they all traveled to Berlin together, where Mendelssohn stayed until he moved to Leipzig for his new position.

As Table 3.3 shows, there are twenty-three movements in MN28, MN53, and MN54 dating from Mendelssohn's initial draft, composed during the first two phases. Of the twenty-three extant movements, eleven movements were eventually cut. Nine of the rejected movements were cut from part 2; only two were taken out of part 1. Of the remaining twelve movements, seven are from part 1 and only five from part 2, which show that the initial draft of part 1 is closer to the performance version than is the initial draft of part 2.

Unfortunately, there is not enough extant material from the first two phases to project the order of movements of the complete draft. The text of several of the extant movements differs from the libretto drafts, suggesting that Mendelssohn rearranged and altered the libretto texts during his composition of the initial draft.

Four movements in MN54 do not date from phases 1 or 2, despite having been written on type A paper. The overture, the *Rachearie* "Vertilge sie," the cavatina "Sei getreu bis in den Tod," and the *Schlußchor* "Nicht aber ihm allein" were inserted into MN54 as part of the revision process of phase 4. There is no obvious explanation why paper of type A was used, because all the other inserted movements of that phase used type B paper. A plausible explanation is that these four movements were the first movements revised in phase 4, after Mendelssohn stopped using type C paper with 12 staves and began using paper with 16 staves instead. Mendelssohn used up the supplies of type A paper with 16 staves and then started using type B paper. Strengthening this hypothesis is the fact that the earlier drafts in MN55 of the *Rachearie* and the cavatina were written on paper of type C. Mendelssohn presumably inserted these two movements toward the end of phase 3.

Phase 3

The third phase began in Berlin in August 1835, where Mendelssohn made his first round of revisions. As the following letter to Moscheles written in August 1835 shows, Mendelssohn was very critical of his work because of his high musical standards:

> But what is the use of grumbling about bad music? As if it could ever take the lead, even if all the world were to sing to it; as if there were no good music left! All such things, however, make me feel the obligation of working hard and of exerting myself to put into the shape to the best of my abilities that which I fancy to be music. I do feel sometimes as if I should never succeed; and to-day I am quite dissatisfied with my work, and should just like to write my Oratorio over again from the beginning to end. But I am quite decided to bring it out at Frankfurt next winter, and at the Düsseldorf Musical Festival at Whitsuntide; so I must finish it now. Besides, I think I have worked too long at it; at least, I am quite impatient to get out other things, so it is evidently high time to end. I have to recopy the whole score, and make a good many alterations and additions—rather a heavy piece of work that often tires me.[12]

From August until November Mendelssohn recopied and revised the first draft of *Paulus*. Although the composer had used type A paper for his first draft, he used paper of type C for all of the parts he rewrote. This paper change becomes evident through a letter by his co-librettist, Schubring, who visited Mendelssohn at the end of September and for whom Mendelssohn must have played through *Paulus*. Schubring made some specific revision suggestions in his letter, dated 8 October 1835, which Mendelssohn followed precisely by discarding several choruses (type A paper) and replacing them with new material (type C paper).[13] By the beginning of November Mendelssohn felt he was close enough to finishing his first round of revisions to discuss its publication with Simrock in a letter written 2 November 1835:

> I am in the process of finishing it [*Paulus*] up, and since you talked to me first about its publication, I take the liberty of letting you know in order to get your ideas on its publication. At first I had the intention to decide about it only after the performance, but it now so happens that the first performance by the *Cäcilienverein* in Frankfurt will be close to the next Music Festival in Düsseldorf (where it probably also will be performed) and with an anticipated performance here. It seems therefore desirable if the publication could happen before the first of these performances, since that would hopefully be advanta-

geous to its dissemination. . . . I think I will be finished with the full score by Christmas.[14]

It is obvious from this letter that the planned performance of *Paulus* in Frankfurt did not take place in the fall of 1835. It was not canceled because Mendelssohn did not think the work to be in performance shape, however. Rather, Schelble had become ill, and the performance was postponed and eventually had to be canceled, because Schelble's health did not improve.

As shown in Table 3.3, most movement drafts in MN53 and MN54 stem from this third phase. When recopying the music, Mendelssohn rewrote most of the score; only the few movements on paper type A did not need enough revision to warrant a new copy.

No mention is made in the correspondence about the writing of the piano-vocal score found in MN55. Since Simrock explained in his response to Mendelssohn's letter, however, that he would like to have a piano-vocal score first, Mendelssohn presumably started work on a piano-vocal score soon after 8 November, the date of the response.[15]

Of the 188 pages of MN55, 132 are written on paper type C; the rest, only 56 pages, are on type B paper. Mendelssohn presumably produced a complete piano-vocal score on type C paper, the same paper used to recopy most of the full score during the third phase. Chapters 4 and 5 show that, while making MN55, Mendelssohn kept revising the music. MN55, therefore, is not merely a copy of the full score but rather an important part of the revision process.

It is impossible to recreate the many stages of the oratorio throughout the revision process of phase 3. Not only are the movements that were replaced in phase 3 missing, but the revisions are too complex to trace, because the revisions of MN53 and MN54 interlock with those of MN55. Essentially every movement has to be viewed separately.

Mendelssohn's work on *Paulus* was sadly interrupted by the death of his father on 19 November 1835. Mendelssohn went back to revising *Paulus* rather quickly, however, because he saw the completion of his first oratorio as an obligation to his deceased father,

> I work now with double zeal on the completion of *Paulus*, since father's last letter urged me on, and since he impatiently awaited the finishing of this work; I feel that I must do everything possible to make it as good as possible, and then imagine that he took part in it. If any good passages come to you, send them to me, you know the course of the whole; I wrote on it today for the first time once again, and will do so daily.[16]

There are not many hints in Mendelssohn's correspondence about when he finished a complete draft of MN53-55 using C type paper. Presumably, he stayed close to his schedule of finishing it by the end of the year.

Phase 4

Phase 4 was the most hectic phase, lasting from the beginning of the year 1836 to the premiere of *Paulus* on 22 May 1836. Mendelssohn must not have been satisfied with his revised draft; he spent another four months on revisions. On 27 February Mendelssohn sent the first part of the piano-vocal score to Simrock:

> Dear Sir,
>   I sent this morning by post the first of the piano-vocal score of my oratorio. I regret, that I had to delay it so long, but the copy that was made took so much time and was also poor when completed, that I had to make many corrections in it, for which I have to ask your pardon. The second part will follow in about two weeks.[17]

Mendelssohn already realized that *Paulus* would need further revisions after the first performance:

> Since it is important to me to have heard the oratorio before the engraving of the piano-vocal score, I wish to wait with it until after the performance, since I will probably want to change more things, for which it would be too late otherwise. I ask you therefore to make for now only engravings of the choral parts, in which I will definitely not have to make any changes. The engraving of the solo parts, if you intend to make them, I would also like to postpone until after the first performance. While I fear that you do not like this, and that you would like to have the piano-vocal score finished for the first performance, it is also in your interest to publish the work in as polished and complete a form as I am able to make it, and I have to admit that it is too important to me that I should not wish to have heard the work first, rather than handing it to the public in definite form with some things in it that are hurried.[18]

Because of the time constraints, Mendelssohn decided to revise the choruses first in order to have the necessary printed choral parts for the premiere. He realized that the solo parts did not need to be mass-produced and therefore need not be printed. Although there are many discrepancies in the recitatives and arias between MN53-54 (which contains the first performance version) and MN55, the choruses show fewer differences. There are still enough differences, however, to suggest that MN55 was not the score used for the printing of the choral parts, which means that at some point MN55 became obsolete, as Mendelssohn worked with another piano-vocal score (probably the one mentioned in his letter from 27 February to Simrock). But there are no discrepancies between the choruses of PS-NYPL and the full score of MN53 and MN54, which suggests that PS-NYPL was copied around the end of February, when Mendelssohn had to send a piano-vocal score for the printing of the choral parts. It is not clear, however, if PS-NYPL was the copy that Mendelssohn sent to Düsseldorf. PS-NYPL could also be the copy made for his mother, which he mentioned in a letter, dated 18 February 1836: "The piano-vocal score of the first part of *Paulus* is being copied for you, dear mother, and I will send it to you shortly."[19]

After more, and at times extensive, revisions of the recitatives and arias, which were not transferred into MN55 or PS-NYPL, on 16 April Mendelssohn sent copies of MN53 and the first part of MN54 to Düsseldorf.[20] A copy of the second part of MN54 followed on 21 April 1836.[21]

Phase 5

> During the whole of the rehearsals and the performance I thought little enough about directing, but listened eagerly to the general effect, and whether it went according to my idea, without thinking of anything else. When the people gave me a flourish of trumpets or applauded, it was welcome for a moment, but then my father came back to my mind, and I strove once more to recall my thoughts to my work. Thus, during the entire performance I was almost in the position of a listener, and tried to retain an impression of the whole. Many parts caused me much pleasure, others not so; but I learnt a lesson from it all, and hope to succeed the next time I write an oratorio.[22]

Two things become clear from this letter about phase 5. First, since *Paulus* was Mendelssohn's first oratorio, he approached his work in an especially critical manner, questioning even his general approach to this genre. Second, his father's death provided strong motivation to refine *Paulus* as much as possible.

After the premiere on 22 May 1836 Mendelssohn spent several more days in Düsseldorf. On 4 June he traveled to Cologne to discuss details of the publication of *Paulus* with Simrock. On 6 June he arrived in Frankfurt to fill in at the *Cäcilienverein* for Schelble, whose health was not getting any better. Over the course of the next two months Mendelssohn revised *Paulus* for the last time, as he prepared the piano-vocal score and full score for publication. Presumably Mendelssohn worked with the copies of MN53-55, which he probably had made for the performance, and which would be much cleaner than MN53-55 themselves. Unfortunately, those scores are no longer extant. Since Mendelssohn now did not have a piano-vocal score containing the revisions that he had entered in MN53 and MN54 after he had sent off the piano-score to Düsseldorf preceding the performance, the making of the piano-vocal score for publication was more time consuming than revising the full score: "I'm truly sorry that you've had such a tough time with the piano arrangement; had you given me even one part of the job, I would have gladly worked on it."[23] Presumably Mendelssohn had to rewrite many of the recitatives and arias, as well as some of the choruses. Consequently, the revision process took him longer than he expected. On 28 June he wrote to Simrock that the sending of the piano-vocal score would have to be delayed.[24] At the end of June Mendelssohn sent the first part of the piano-vocal score to Simrock, and on 2 July the full score of part 1.[25] On 23 July the full score and piano-vocal score of part 2 without the *Schlußchor* was sent;[26] the final chorus was finished soon thereafter.

Notes

1. Felix Mendelssohn, Düsseldorf, to Abraham Mendelssohn, Berlin, ALS, 28 March 1834, New York Public Library: Auch hat der Paulus schon ziemlich Fortschritte gemacht und ich denke schon vor Pfingsten mit dem Schreiben anfangen zu können.

2. Felix Mendelssohn, *Felix Mendelssohn-Bartholdys Briefwechsel mit Legationsrat Karl Klingemann in London*, ed. Karl Klingemann Jr. (Essen: G.D. Baedeker, 1909), 130: Mein Oratorium ist angefangen und ich habe sonst viel zu tun und zu arbeiten, bin also wohl.

3. Felix Mendelssohn, Leipzig, to Lea Mendelssohn, Berlin, ALS, 2 May 1834, New York Public Library: Mein Oratorium ist angefangen, 2 Nummern schon fertig, und ich hoffe gewiß bis zum Herbst wenigstens den ersten Theil beendigt zu haben, vielleicht mehr.

4. Felix Mendelssohn, *Letters of Felix Mendelssohn to Ignaz and Charlotte Moscheles*, ed. and trans. by Felix Moscheles (Boston: Ticknor, 1888), 11 May 1834, 109.

5. Felix Mendelssohn, Leipzig, to Lea Mendelssohn, Berlin, ALS, 6 June 1834, New York Public Library: Ich arbeite jetzt ziemlich viel, und befinde mich prächtig wohl. Einige neue Chöre vom Paulus habe ich seitdem gemacht, ob aber Schelble, wie er es verlangt, das Oratorium schon im nächsten Winter aufführen kann, das bezweifle ich stark, doch habe ich noch nicht geantwortet, und es soll vom Erfolg meiner Arbeit in den nächsten Wochen abhängen.

6. Felix Mendelssohn, *Letters from 1833 to 1847*, ed. Paul and Carl Mendelssohn-Bartholdy; trans. by Lady Wallace (London: Longman, Green and Co., 1890), 39-40.

7. Felix Mendelssohn, *Felix Mendelssohn-Bartholdys Briefwechsel mit Legationsrat Karl Klingemann in London*, 30 November 1834, 157.

8. Felix Mendelssohn, *Felix Mendelssohn-Bartholdys Briefwechsel mit Legationsrat Karl Klingemann in London*, 30 November 1834, 154-55: Erst seitdem bin ich auch wieder an die Arbeit gekommen, aber mit welcher Lust! . . . Dumm ist es freilich, dass ich jetzt die Aufforderung bekomme mein Oratorium zum Pfingstfest in Cöln aufzuführen, und dass ich es der versäumten Zeit wegen abschlagen muss; hätt ich die zwei Monate gearbeitet, die ich verloren habe, so hätte ich's aufführen können. . . .

9. Mendelssohn, 170: So total einsam, wenigstens geistig oder musikalisch, wie diesen Winter hier, habe ich noch gar nicht gelebt. Ich sehe den einen 15. nach dem andern heranschleichen, und merke, dass etwas dazwischen liegt, nur an der immer anwachsenden Bogenzahl meines Oratoriums, und der abnehmenden des leeren Notenpapiers aus Berlin.

10. Felix Mendelssohn, *Felix Mendelssohn-Bartholdys Briefwechsel mit Legationsrat Karl Klingemann in London*, 26 March 1835, 173: Im Anfang suchte ich die Reise im Mai immer noch festzuhalten, aber endlich ging's nicht mehr, und das sollte ich Dir nach 14 Tagen geschrieben haben und verschob es von einem zum andern. Erst dehnte sich das Oratorium aus, und wird vor der Mitte Mai schwerlich fertig werden. . . . Nun macht sich's auch so, dass Hensels wahrscheinlich zum Musikfest gerade herkommen, dann einige Tage in Düsseldorf bleiben, viel zu arbeiten gibt es obendrein für das Fest, kurz, ich muss, um mein Oratorium ganz fertig zu bekommen und zugleich die Direktion nicht zu vernachlässigen, bis zum Juni auf jeden Fall hier bleiben. Zugleich hat mir Schelble von Frankfurt geschrieben, dass er den Paulus im Oktober oder November zum ersten Male zu geben wünscht, also habe ich mir vorgenommen, nach dem Musikfeste ihm die Partitur nach Frankfurt zu bringen, alle Rücksprache mit ihm zu nehmen, und dann (im Juli also) einige Wochen zu reisen, nach der Schweiz, oder England, oder zu den Eltern.

11. Mendelssohn, 17 April 1835, 178: Ich lebe sehr still und allein, oft spreche ich mit keinem Menschen am ganzen Tage soviel als mit meinem Pferd. Dabei rückt das Oratorium nach und nach vor, und sobald es fertig ist, sollen die Sinfonien heran.

12. Felix Mendelssohn, *Letters of Felix Mendelssohn to Ignaz and Charlotte Moscheles*, 136-37.

13. See chapter 5, pp. 234-35, for a detailed description of these revisions.

14. Felix Mendelssohn, *Briefe an deutsche Verleger*, ed. Rudolf Elvers (Berlin: Walter de Gruyter & Co., 1968), 196: Ich bin jetzt aber damit beschäftigt die letzte Hand daran [*Paulus*] zu legen, und da Sie mir zuerst von der Herausgabe desselben gesprochen haben, so erlaube ich mir auch Sie zuerst davon zu benachrichtigen, um Ihre Ansichten über die Publication zu erfahren. Ich hatte früher nämlich die Absicht mich erst nach der Aufführung darüber zu entscheiden, und hätte dies wohl auch gethan, wenn es sich nicht jetzt träfe, daß die erste Aufführung im Cäcilien-Verein zu Frankfurt, mit dem nächsten Musikfest in Düsseldorf (wo es auch wahrscheinlich gegeben wird) und mit einer hier beabsichtigten Aufführung nahe zusammen fällt. Deshalb scheint es mir für die Herausgabe wünschenswerth wenn sie *vor* der ersten dieser Aufführungen geschehen könnte, da das der Verbreitung hoffentlich günstig wäre. . . . Bis gegen Weihnachten gedenke ich mit der ganzen Partitur fertig zu sein.

15. Mendelssohn, 198.

16. Felix Mendelssohn, *Briefwechsel zwischen Felix Mendelssohn und J. Schubring zugleich ein Beitrag zur Geschichte des Oratoriums*, ed. Julius Schubring (Leipzig: Duncker & Humblot, 1892), 6 December 1835, 99-100: Überhaupt mache ich mich nun mit doppeltem Eifer an die Vollendung des Paulus, da der letzte Brief des Vaters mich dazu trieb, und er in der letzten Zeit sehr ungeduldig die Beendigung dieser Arbeit erwartete; mir ists, als müßte ich nun alles anwenden, um Paulus so gut als möglich zu vollenden, und mir dann denken, er nähme Theil daran. Fallen dir noch gute Stellen auf, so schicke sie mir noch, Du kennst ja den Gang des Ganzen; ich habe heute wieder zum erstenmale wieder daran geschrieben, und will es nun täglich thun.

17. Felix Mendelssohn, *Briefe an deutsche Verleger*, 200: Ew. Wohlgeboren habe ich diesen Morgen mit der Fahrpost den ersten Theil des Clavierauszuges meines Oratoriums zugeschickt. Ich bedaure, daß ich damit so lange zögern mußte, aber die Abschrift die ich machen ließ hielt mich so sehr auf und ich fand sie nach der Beendigung so mangelhaft, daß ich unendlich viele Correcturen darin zu machen hatte, und auch deshalb um Entschuldigung bitten muß. In etwa 14 Tagen soll noch der fehlende zweite Theil ebenfalls nachkommen.

18. Mendelssohn, 200-201: Da es mir sehr darum zu thun wäre, das Oratorium erst einmal gehört zu haben, ehe der Stich des Clavierauszugs vorgenommen würde, so wünsche ich, daß derselbe bis *nach* der Aufführung verschoben würde, da ich doch wahrscheinlich noch manches würde ändern wollen, wozu es hernach zu spät wäre. Ich bitte sie also für jetzt nur die Chorstimmen stechen zu lassen, in den auf keinen Fall später noch Abänderungen zu machen sein werden. Den Stich der Solostimmen, wenn Sie ihn beabsichtigen, wünsche ich aber ebenfalls bis nach der ersten Aufführung verschoben zu haben. Obwohl ich fürchten muß, daß die Ihnen nicht ganz recht ist, und daß Sie bei den ersten Aufführungen lieber schon den Clavierauszug fertig hätten, so wird doch auch Ihnen daran liegen, das Werk so abgerundet und vollendet, als ich es vermag,

erscheinen zu sehen, und ich gestehe Ihnen daß es mir zu wichtig ist als daß ich nicht wünschen sollte es erst selbst gehört zu haben, ehe ich es der Öffentlichkeit definitiv übergeben möchte, und etwas dabei übereilte.

19. Felix Mendelssohn, Leipzig, to Lea Mendelssohn, Berlin, ALS, 18 February 1836, New York Public Library: Den Clavierauszug des ersten Theiles vom Paulus laße ich bereits für dich abschreiben liebe Mutter und werde ihn dir bald zuschicken.

20. Felix Mendelssohn, Leipzig, to the Committee of the Lower Rhine Music Festival, Düsseldorf, ALS, 16 April 1836, Heinrich-Heine-Institut Düsseldorf, Musikvereinsdepos. letter 13; quoted in chapter 2 on p. 23.

21. Felix Mendelssohn, Leipzig, to Ferdinand von Woringen, Düsseldorf, ALS, 30 March 1836, Heinrich-Heine-Institut Düsseldorf, Musikvereinsdepos. letter 15.

22. Felix Mendelssohn, *Letters from 1833 to 1847*, to Conrad Schleinitz, 5 July 1836, 105.

23. Fanny Hensel, *The Letters of Fanny Hensel to Felix Mendelssohn*, ed. and trans. by Marcia J. Citron (New York: Pendragon Press, 1987), 30 July 1836, 208.

24. Felix Mendelssohn, *Briefe an deutsche Verleger*, 203-204.

25. Mendelssohn, 204-205.

26. Mendelssohn, 206.

Chapter 4

Compositional Process in Individual Movements of Part 1

Overture

Chronology

The overture to *Paulus* seems to have been one of the most difficult movements for Mendelssohn to write. He did not attempt to compose the overture until after he arrived at the antepenultimate movement of the first part:

> By the way, I feel very melancholy today, as I have been the past several days, when I was completely unproductive, not having written anything; if it is the heat or the humidity, I do not know. The first part of *Paulus* is almost finished now, and I stand in front of it like a cow and cannot enter the new gate, cannot finish it—the overture is still missing, and it is a difficult piece. Right after the words of the Lord at the conversion I entered a big chorus, "Mache dich auf, werde Licht," etc., Is. 60:1-2, which I regard as the best moment of the first part so far.[1]

Mendelssohn's obvious hesitation to write the overture for his first oratorio might stem from a comment made by Schubring almost a year earlier, on 5 October 1833, about the function of an overture:

I find an opening chorus necessary; an overture less so. The Handelian type of adagio and fugue seems overdone, it tends to have no real
content (not always). I also think that you musicians easily fall into
the temptation to get absorbed in the music, over which the spiritual
meaning of the oratorio gets lost. But if you have something in mind
that fits, something that could refer to the time of the first congregation before Stephen's death—a Pentecost, where the Holy Spirit is
poured out—according to Acts 2; which contains much musical material. There are also other passages such as Acts 2:42-47 or 4:32, or
passages that refer to the continuous persecution of chapters 4 and 5,
where also the power of God and the prayer of the Church is shown,
Acts 4:24-31. If you could like such an idea, it would make a good
introduction to an opening chorus of the kind I suggested earlier. Of
course, an overture could also contain references to such a piece.[2]

Mendelssohn was unsure about the function, content, and form of the
overture. Schubring's suggestion of a programmatic orchestral opening
instead of a conventional overture, however, must have seemed difficult to realize. Although Mendelssohn decided to use a conventional
French overture after all, the use of the chorale "Wachet auf! ruft uns
die Stimme" ties the overture effectively to the body of the oratorio,
especially since the chorale reappears later in the oratorio. Perhaps
Mendelssohn thought of using the chorale "Wachet auf!" while he was
working on the last scene of part 1 of the oratorio. It is hardly a coinci-
dence that Mendelssohn started to compose the overture precisely at the
time when he reached the place where the chorale reappears in the oratorio, after the chorus "Mache dich auf, werde Licht."

Even after Mendelssohn decided to write the overture, it took another three months until he actually started work on it. He wrote to his
sister Fanny on 14 November 1834, "In recent days I have sketched the
overture for *St. Paul*, and I thought of finishing it at least, but work is
far behind schedule."[3] This was the last mention of the compositional
process of the overture.

Revision Stages

MN53 and MN55 bear witness to a slow compositional process. Both
sources show revisions within themselves as well as in comparison to
each other and to the Simrock version. Table 4.1 shows the revision
stages of the overture.

Table 4.1. Revision Stages of the Overture

1. MN55I					
2. MN55II					
PS-NYPL					
3. MN53I	[x-8]	+	9-12ac	+	[13-y]
4. MN53II	3-8ac	+	9-12pc	+	[13-Y]
5. MN53II	3-8ac	+	9-12pc	+	13-20ac
6. MN53III	3-20pc				
7. Simrock					

Determining the chronological order of MN53 and MN55 is very simple, because MN53 comes much closer to the printed version than does MN55, and Mendelssohn invalidated this version by crossing out the first pages of the "Primo" and "Secondo" parts. Also, as already discussed in previous chapters, the orchestral score of MN53 was put together by Mendelssohn shortly before the first performance—much later than the piano-vocal score of MN55.

While the revision process of MN55 is very simple, since all the corrections were made in the music without any insertions, it nevertheless seems almost impossible to retrace completely Mendelssohn's revision process within the manuscript sources. Not only is the overture in MN53 written on two different types of paper, but there is also an insertion of a single sheet within type A, indicating a multilayered revision process (see Table 4.2).

Table 4.2 shows that the first system of the folio containing pages 9-12 is crossed out (except for the last measure). The last system of page 8 shows a revised version of this discarded section. This suggests that the bifolio consisting of pages 9-12 originated from an earlier version; the first six pages (pp. 3-8) of the overture replaced the opening of the earlier version leading up to pages 9-12. The remaining two bifolios are both B paper types. Since there is no crossed-out section on either bifolio 9-12 or bifolio 13-16, one must assume that the B-bifolios were also written during a fairly advanced revision stage.

Table 4.2. Foliation and Paper Type of the Overture in MN53

Page number	Comments	Paper type
3	first page of music; "Hilf Du mir"	A
[4]		A
5		A
[6]		A
7		AT
[8]		AT
9	first 9 mm. Crossed out	AT
[10]		AT
11		AT
[12]		AT
13		B
[14]		B
15		B
[16]		B
17		B
[18]		B
19		B
[20]		B

Revisions

A comparison of the different versions of the overture shows that, while the overall formal design was already established in the two earliest versions represented by MN55, the composition nevertheless underwent numerous revisions. The degrees of revision range from minor changes in instrumentation and voicing to the complete replacement of sections. The most thorough revision process took place between MN55II and MN53I; all of the other versions of Table 4.1—including the printed Simrock version—show less severe revisions of their immediately preceding versions. The discussion that follows presents some examples of the different types of revisions.

In the slow introduction Mendelssohn's revisions focused on the section immediately following the chorale. In MN55I (Example 4.1a) he wrote three 4-measure phrases with a clear closing character, which lead back to the final phrase of the chorale played twice to close out the slow introduction. Mendelssohn must have felt that these three closing-type phrases were unmotivated and that they slowed the pace of the composition down too much. He crossed out the three 4-measure phrases and one statement of the final chorale phrase (mm. 28-43). This

Example 4.1a. MN55, Overture, mm. 25-48

solution creates a short, plain, and slow introduction, however,simply stating the chorale tune. In MN53 Mendelssohn added once again a closing section following the statement of the chorale (see Example 4.1b). By letting the new material grow out of the accompaniment of the chorale and avoiding a final cadence in the chorale (see mm. 25-27), he was able to keep the introduction moving forward toward a much more convincing cadence.

Example 4.1b. MN53/Simrock, Overture 25-43

The following fast fugal section shows numerous contrapuntal revisions; again, the most drastic corrections take place between stages 2
and 3 of Table 4.1. A comparison of the fugal expositions (see Examples 4.2a and b) exemplifies the kinds of contrapuntal revisions Mendelssohn made. The basic structure is the same; the voices enter in the
same order, and the subjects are very similar. Mendelssohn made many

Example 4.2a. MN53, Overture—fugal exposition

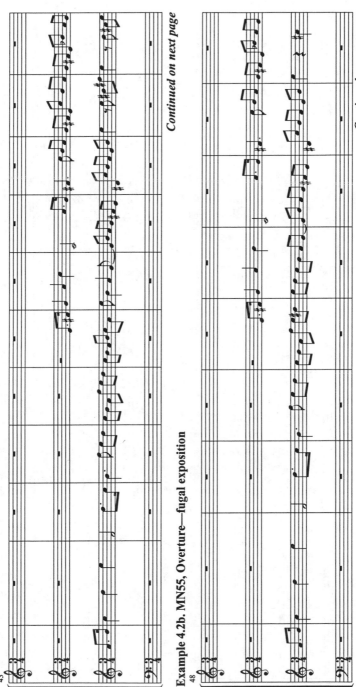

Continued on next page

Example 4.2b. MN55, Overture—fugal exposition

Continued on next page

(Example 4.2a—Continued)

(Example 4.2b—Continued)

contrapuntal changes, however. The entrances between the statements of the subject are each delayed by one measure in MN53. This seems an unusual revision for Mendelssohn, who usually made the structure in his revisions more compact. A closer look, however, reveals that this delay is part of Mendelssohn's attempt to make this exposition more transparent. Whenever the subject enters in MN53, the other voices slow down rhythmically, making the subject stand out more clearly. Through the delay of the entrances Mendelssohn slowed down the harmonic rhythm, which makes the longer note values at entrances possible. As a result, the listener is better able to follow the exposition.

Between all stages of revision Mendelssohn, as expected, tightened the structure of the overture by taking out measures. These short, one- or two-measure cuts come mostly at the ends of transitional sections, making a quicker, more focused move into the next section. The only exception is the more substantial revision from MN53 to Simrock of the transition from the first fugal theme to the second (MN53, mm. 71-85; Simrock, mm. 71-77). The composer cut eight measures and made the necessary adjustments to achieve a quicker transition.

Opening

Revision Stages

The side-by-side comparison in Table 4.3 of the text portions of each source of the opening shows the gradual process that the opening went through until it reached its published form. Although the libretto stages are easy to compare, the stages of revision of the music, especially in MN53 and MN55, are very complex, because there are several layers of revisions in those manuscripts.

Libretto Revisions

Mendelssohn's initial idea of a chorus of the disciples as they gather together was never abandoned in any of the stages. Schubring's draft suggests two scripture passages, Psalm 23:1-4 and Psalm 46:2-4. Marx's choice of Psalm 46:2-4 over Psalm 23 in his draft is not surprising; the imagery of God's sustaining power as being stronger than any natural catastrophe makes a better opening for Marx's drama-oriented plot than the lyric and idyllic metaphors of Psalm 23. Mendelssohn,

Table 4.3. Sources of the Opening of Part 1

Libretto sources

FMB—MDM c.42	Schubring—d. 30, no. 214	Fürst—d. 53, no. 87; d. 30, no. 211	Marx—d. 53, no. 88	FMB—d.30, no. 211; Schubring's comments	FMB—c. 27, p. 28r-30v
Chor der Jünger in ihrer Gemeinschaft—unspecified	1. Chor der Christen "Gott ist unsere Zuversicht und Stärke," or "Der Herr ist mein Hirte"	Chor "Herr, der du bist der Gott"	Chor "Gott ist unsere Zuversicht und Stärke"	suggestions of Bible verses by Schubring from Acts, chapters 2, 4, and 5.	Chor "Herr, der Du bist der Gott"
	1. Autrement. "Ach bleib mit deiner Gnade"				Choral "Ach bleib mit deiner Gnade"

Musical sources

MN19	MN28	MN55	PS-NYPL	MN53ac	MN53pc	Program of premier	Simrock
sketch of opening of "Herr, der du bist der Gott"		2. Chor "Herr, der du bist der Gott"	2. Chor "Herr, der du bist der Gott"	2. Choral "Allein Gott in der Höh sei Ehr"	2. Chor "Herr, der du bist der Gott"	2. Chor "Herr, der du bist der Gott"	2. Coro "Herr, der du bist der Gott"
	2. Choral "Ach bleib mit deiner Gnade"	3. Rec. "Die Menge der Gläubigen"	3. Rec. "Die Menge der Gläubigen"	4. Recativo "Die Menge der Gläubigen/Stephanus aber"	3. Rec. "Die Menge der Gläubigen"	3. Rec. "Die Menge der Gläubigen"	3. Choral "Allein Gott in der Höh sei Ehr"
	3. Rec. "Die Menge der Gläubigen"	4. Choral "Allein Gott in der Höh sei Ehr"	4. Choral "Allein Gott in der Höh sei Ehr"		4. Choral "Allein Gott in der Höh sei Ehr"	4. Choral "Allein Gott in der Höh sei Ehr"	4. Recativo "Die Menge der Gläubigen/Stephanus aber"

Source: Sposato, Jeffrey, Mendelssohn's Theological Evolution: A Study of Textual Choice and Change in the Composer's Sacred Works, Ph.D. diss., Brandeis University, 1999.

however, was not satisfied with either of the two suggestions; the second draft lacks an opening chorus as well as a chorale. Schubring, in his letter of 5 October 1833, quoted previously, suggested a programmatic orchestral opening movement based on events from the book of Acts. While Mendelssohn decided against a programmatic orchestral opening movement, he did not reject Schubring's suggestions completely. In his third draft (c. 27, pp. 28r-30v), Mendelssohn followed Schubring's textual suggestions and used parts of Acts 4:24, 26, and 29 as the text for his opening chorus. The fact that some of Schubring's suggestions of Bible verses were the same as Fürst's suggestion for an opening chorus (see Table 4.3) might have helped Mendelssohn in the choice of his text. Mendelssohn, however, made his own selection of verses for the opening chorus. He carefully chose three verses; each verse contains an important element for the setting of the stage for the entire oratorio. Acts 4:24 proclaims the faith of the disciples in God the Creator; Acts 4:26 expresses the world's adversity against Christ; and Acts 4:29 shows the determination to spread the Gospel, as well as the dependence on God in this endeavor.

In his third draft (c. 27, pp. 28r-30v) Mendelssohn also followed Schubring's suggestion of "Ach bleib mit deiner Gnade" as the first chorale. MN28 contains the only musical setting of that chorale. There is some evidence to suggest that this chorale setting in MN28 must have been part of a very early version, possibly based on Mendelssohn's third draft. The chorale setting uses the same three stanzas as the first c. 27 draft does, which Mendelssohn selected from the six stanzas supplied by Schubring in his first draft. Moreover, this setting is very different from all the other settings; it is not just composed in cantional style with instruments doubling the vocal parts; rather, it is treated like a chorus with independent instrumental lines.

While Mendelssohn kept the text of the opening chorus from the first c. 27 draft on, the choice of the chorale changed. Starting with the MN53I version he decided on "Allein Gott in der Höh sei Ehr." Unlike "Ach bleib mit deiner Gnade," which focuses on God's sustaining grace, "Allein Gott in der Höh sei Ehr" is a hymn of praise, which Mendelssohn seemed to have felt would make a better first chorale.

In all the music sources Mendelssohn added a recitative to the opening section of the oratorio. The earliest stage containing a recitative text is MN53I, where the recitative appears as the fourth movement. Only the first part of the recitative text pertains to the opening section, "Die Menge der Gläubigen war ein Herz und eine Seele, und das Wort Gottes nahm zu" (Acts 4:32/6:7). The text then leads into the first scene, introducing Stephen: "Stephanus aber, voll Glauben . . ."

(Acts 6:8-13). The recitative is followed by a duet, in which Stephen is accused. In MN53II Mendelssohn not only discarded the recitative by crossing it out, but he changed the constellation of the opening by creating two separate recitatives with longer texts; one before the chorale, belonging to the opening, and one after the chorale, belonging to the first scene. The reason that the discarded recitative No. 4 of MN53I was left in MN53 was simply to save paper. The folio that contains the crossed out No. 4 also contains the ensuing duet, which Mendelssohn did not want to discard. After the performance Mendelssohn decided that he liked the idea of the combined recitative better than the two separate ones and went back to the text of MN53I.

Musical Revisions

The first musical traces of the chorus "Herr, der du bist der Gott" can be found in MN19.[4] The first page contains a thematic sketch of 36 measures (see Example 4.3). The sketch already begins with the three introductory chords found in all of the versions of the opening chorus. The motive of "der du bist der Gott" shares only the rhythm with the later version. The rest of the sketch of MN19 is different from the drafts.

Starting with MN53, the chorus "Herr, der Du bist der Gott" underwent five traceable revisions; because of the replacement of folios and the insertion of single pages, however, not all six stages can be recreated (see Table 4.4). It is evident that the last bifolio of "Herr, der Du bist der Gott" (pp. 39-42) is from an earlier version than the preceding ones, since the whole first page of the last bifolio is crossed out. The crossed-out page contains the end of a transitional section. Mendelssohn, as was often the case in his corrections, decided to simplify this transition harmonically and melodically (see Examples 4.4a and b). There are two other instances of revisions of transitional sections similar to the corrections shown above (MN53IV mm.71-75, Simrock mm. 70-71; MN53IV mm. 84-88, Simrock mm. 79-82). In the first section the composer cut four measures; in the second section he once again simplified the counterpoint in order to gain clarity.

The only single page in this chorus (29-30) stems also from an earlier version, as is evident from the fact that it has been corrected much more heavily than the two bifolios on either side. Of course, it is impossible to know whether pages 29-30 and 39-42 actually are from the same version. Mendelssohn probably revised the opening up to the single page at some point and was able to reuse this half-folio.

Example 4.3. MN19, "Herr, der du bist der Gott" I—sketch

Table 4.4. Revision Stages of "Herr, der du bist der Gott"

1. MN53II	[xx-28]	+	29-30ac	+	[31-38]	+	39-42ac
2. MN53III	21-28ac	+	29-30pc	+	[31-38]	+	39-42pc
3. MN55I	9-17ac						
4. MN53IV	21-30pc	+			31-38ac	+	39-42pc
4a. MN53IVa	21-30pc	+			31-38pc	+	39-42pc
5. PS-NYPL							
6. Simrock							

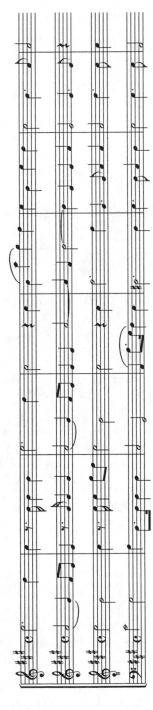

Example 4.4a. MN53, "Herr, der du bist der Gott" II—mm. 126-33

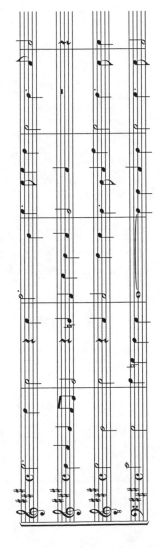

Example 4.4b. MN53, "Herr, der du bist der Gott" II—mm. 121-25, 133

The two bifolios containing pages 31-38 are very interesting. There is only one cross-out in the vocal parts, which actually reflects a copying error by Mendelssohn. He copied the vocal bass entrance one measure too early and had to cross it out (see Figure 4.1). The other few corrections are in the instrumental parts. Perhaps Mendelssohn replaced these two bifolios after he had already written the piano-vocal score, because there are corrections in the piano-vocal score that he transferred into the clean orchestral score.

There are three main types of corrections found in MN53 and MN55. One is the revoicing of chords; the second is the smoothing-out of melodic lines; and the third is the increase of transparency in texture.

The revoicing can be seen in the opening chords (see Examples 4.5a-c). The earlier version started with c#"-e"-f#" in the soprano as the top notes of the chords. In order to bring out the third chord and raise the intensity level with each chord, Mendelssohn altered the voicing, changing the soprano line to a'-c#"-f#". In the printed version it is changed yet again to e"-a'-f#"; the large leaps raise the intensity level even more in comparison to the earlier version.

The smoothing-out of the individual vocal parts can be seen most clearly in MN53 (see Examples 4.6a and b). Mendelssohn changed the melodic line generally to avoid unnecessary leaps. To gain transparency, Mendelssohn at times thinned out the contrapuntal texture, bringing out the vocal part with the important motivic material.

A comparison of the recitatives of MN53II, MN53III, MN55I, and MN55II/PS-NYPL leaves unanswered questions. MN55II/PS-NYPL is the corrected version of MN55I; both of these versions, however, differ slightly from the versions found in MN53, even though neither version shows corrections in these spots. This is especially remarkable, since in measure 7 Mendelssohn made the same corrections in both scores, showing his attempt to keep these two versions the same. In the printed version the recitative is completely reworked, leaving only a few musical similarities with the old no. 4.

Figure 4.1 MN53, p. 32.

Example 4.5a. MN53ac/55ac, "Herr, der du bist der Gott" III

Example 4.5b. MN53pc/55pc, "Herr, der du bist der Gott" III

Example 4.5c. Simrock, "Herr, der du bist der Gott" III

Example 4.6a. MN53ac, "Herr, der du bist der Gott" IV

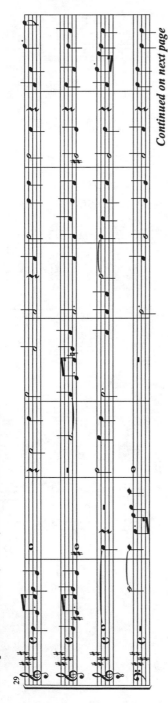

Continued on next page

Example 4.6b. MN53pc, "Herr, der du bist der Gott" IV

Continued on next page

(Example 4.6a—*Continued*)

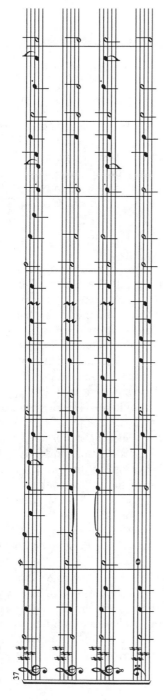

(Example 4.6b—*Continued*)

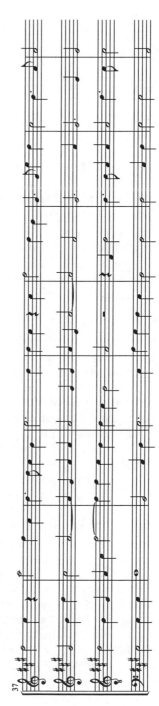

Capture, Trial, and the Stoning of Stephen

Overview

The first scene of the oratorio consists of three parts: Stephen's capture and accusations, the trial with Stephen's sermon, and his stoning (see Table 4.5). As was the case with the opening, the basic structure of the libretto was already in place in Mendelssohn's first outline in his letter of 22 December 1832 to Schubring. Throughout all the complete libretto drafts the tripartite structure of this scene remained intact.

Capture and Accusations

The recitative that opens the scene does not show as many revisions as some of the other movements. This can partially be explained by the fact that Mendelssohn added it into the score fairly late in the compositional process. As discussed earlier, in MN53 Mendelssohn had the recitative positioned differently and divided it into two parts. The versions of MN53 and MN55 are nearly identical—including their corrections. All the revisions are minor; they are all concerned with the smoothing-out of the vocal line. The Simrock version is quite different from the earlier versions. Because Mendelssohn went back to the idea of the contracted recitative as found crossed out in MN53, there are obviously some major differences from the revised versions of MN53 and MN55. The recitative in the printed version starts in E major, the key of the preceding chorale; in MN53 and MN55 the key shifts abruptly to G major. In the Simrock version the music avoids the jump in keys and then eventually modulates to the E minor of the following bass duet, which became possible as a result of the longer text. After the modulation Mendelssohn retained the earlier version of MN53/55.

The revision process of the bass duet "Wir haben ihn gehört" and the recitative "Und bewegten das Volk" in MN53 can be traced better than that of the previous recitative, because it dates back to an earlier compositional stage. MN53 contains the earliest version; MN55 is a transcription of MN53 with some revisions. The revisions in MN53 of "Wir haben ihn gehört" are mainly in the accompaniment. Mendelssohn lightened the texture by reducing the orchestra as well as by the omission of some of the faster runs (see Figure 4.2). At the end of the duet Mendelssohn cut the penultimate measure, which contained a text repetition.

Table 4.5. Sources of Part 1, Scene 1

		Libretto sources			
FMB—MDM c.42	Schubring—d. 30, no. 214	Fürst—d. 53, no. 87; d. 30, no. 211	Marx—d. 53, no. 88	FMB—d.30, no. 211; Schubring's comments	FMB—c. 27, 28r-30v
		Capture and Accusation			
Stephanus gefangen (Acts 6:8-13)	2. Stephanus aber (Acts 6:8 ff.)	Stephanus: Murret nicht (Joh. 6:43)	Rec.: "Stephanus aber"	[Rec.:] "Stephanus aber voll Glaubens"	Choral: "Ach bleib mit deiner Gnade"
Zeu-gen gegen ihn	3. So aber das Amt (2. Cor. 3:7, 8)	Volk: "Mache dich auf, Gott" (Ps. 74: 22)	Chor: "Haben wir diesen Menschen nicht"	Chor: "Dieser Mensch"	Rec.: "Stephanus voll Glaubens"
		Andern: "Der Herr ist" (Nah. 1:2)	Rec.: "Da richteten sie zu";		Chor: "Dieser Mensch"
			Solostimmen: "Wir haben ihn gehört"		
		Zeugen: "Wir haben diesen Stephanus"	Chor: "Was sollte Gott nach jenem fragen"		
			Rec.: "Und traten herzu"		
			Arie: "Gottes Zorn vom Himmel"		
			Rec.: "Und stellten fal-sche Zeugen";		
			Solostimmen: "Dieser Mensch hört nicht auf"		
			Chor: "Weg, weg mit ihm"		

Continued on next page

(Table 4.5—Continued)

FMB—MDM c.42	Schubring—d.30, no. 214	Fürst—d. 53, no. 87; d. 30, no. 211	Marx—d. 53, no. 88	FMB—d.30, no. 211; Schubring's comments	FMB—c. 27, 28r-30v
Trial					
Steph. Predigt (Acts 7:2, 48-53)	4. Er aber sprach: Ihr Halsstarrigen (Acts 7:2, 51)	Stephanus: "Läster-worte wider Moses?" Arie: "Ihr Halsstarrigen"	Rec: "Und sie sahen auf ihn alle"	[Rec.:] "Und sie sahen auf ihn alle"	Rec.: "Und sie sahen auf ihn alle"
Chor: sie bissen die Zähne zusammen	5. Herr, verflucht sein alle (Tob. 13:15)	Schriftgelehrten: "Er klage es" (Ps. 22:9)	Stephanus: "Liebe Brüder und Väter"		Chor: "Hinweg mit solchem"
Steph. (Acts 7:55)	6. Als er aber voll heiligen Geistes war (Acts 7:55)	Stephanus: "Siehe, ich sehe den Himmel"; Hoherath: "Weg mit ihm"	Rec.: "Da sie solches höreten"; Chor: "Weg, weg mit dem!"	[Stephanus:] "Siehe ich sehe den Himmel"	[Stephanus:] "Sie-he ich sehe den Himmel offen"
	7. Denn er selbst, der Herr (1. Thess. 4:16)	Jünger: "Hinweg mit sol-chem" Jünger: "Siehe, sie halten des Herrn Wort"	Rec.: "Als er aber voll heiligen Geistes war" Stephanus: "Siehe, ich sehe den Himmel offen"	Chor: "Steiniget ihm"	Chor: "Steiniget ihm"
Stoning					
Chor: Acts 7:56	8. Sie schrieen aber laut (Act. 7:56)	Stephanus: "Herr Jesu nimm meinen Geist auf"	Chor: "Steiniget ihm!"	Chor: "Steiniget ihm"	[Rec.:] "Sie hielten aber ihre Ohren zu"
	9. "Weg, weg mit dem"	Saulus und Volk: "Also müssen umkommen"	Rec.: "Sie schrien aber"	[Rec.:] "Und die Zeugen"	Aria: "Der du die Menschen"
	10. "Und sie stießen ihn"	Inger: "Sieh, wir preisen selig"	Chor: "Da! Da!" Rec.: "Und steinigten ihn"	[Steph.:] "Herr behalte ih-nen diese Sünde nicht."	Choral: ~~"Erscheine mir zum Schilde"~~
	11. "Gott mache sie"	Paulus: "Gott wird den Kopf"	Stephanus: "Herr, behalte Ihnen diese Sünde nicht."	[Rec.:] ~~"Und die Zeugen"~~	
	12. "Und sie steinigten"	Jünger: "Gott ist unsere Zuversicht und Stärke"	Rec.: "Und als er das gesagt" Chor: "Ach Bruder!"	Aria: "Gott mache sie wie einen Wirbel"	

Continued on next page

(Table 4.5—Continued)

		Musical sources			
MN55	PS-NYPL	MN53ac	MN53pc	Program of premier	Simrock
Capture and Accusations					
5. Rec.: "Stephanus aber"; Duet: "Wir haben ihn gehört"; Rec.: "Da bewegten sie das Volk"	5. Rec.: "Stephanus aber"; Duet: "Wir haben ihn gehört"; Rec.: "Da bewegten sie das Volk"		5. Rec.: "Stephanus aber"; Duet: "Wir haben ihn gehört"; Rec.: "Und bewegten das Volk"	5. Rec.: "Stephanus aber"; Duet: "Wir haben ihn gehört"; Rec.: "Und bewegten das Volk"	4b. Rec.: "Stephanus aber"; Duet: "Wir haben ihn gehört"; Rec.: "Und bewegten das Volk"
6. Chor: "Dieser Mensch"	6. Chor: "Dieser Mensch"	4. Chor.: "Dieser Mensch"	6. Chor: "Dieser Mensch"	6. Chor: "Dieser Mensch"	5. Coro: "Dieser Mensch"
Trial					
7. Rec.: "Und sie sahen auf ihn alle"; Chor: "Weg, weg mit dem"	7. Rec.: "Und sie sahen auf ihn alle"; Chor: "Weg, weg mit dem"	5. Rec.: "Und sie sahen auf ihn alle"; Chor: "Weg, weg mit dem"	7. Rec.: "Und sie sahen auf ihn alle"; Chor: "Weg, weg mit dem"	7. Rec.: "Und sie sahen auf ihn alle"; Chor: "Weg, weg mit dem"	6. Rec.: "Und sie sahen auf ihn alle"; Coro: "Weg, weg mit dem"
8. Arioso: "Jerusalem"	8. Arioso: "Jerusalem"	6. Aria: "Jerusalem"	8. Aria: "Jerusalem"	8. Arie: "Jerusalem"	7. Aria: "Jerusalem"
9. Rec.: "Sie aber stürmten auf ihn ein"; Chor: "Steiniget ihn"	9. Rec.: "Sie aber stürmten auf ihn ein"; Chor: "Steiniget ihn"	7. Rec.: "Sie aber stürmten auf ihn ein"; Chor: "Steiniget ihn"	9. Rec.: "Sie aber stürmten auf ihn ein"; Chor: "Steiniget ihn"	9. Rec.: "Sie aber stürmten auf ihn ein"; Chor: "Steiniget ihn"	8. Rec.: "Sie aber stürmten auf ihn ein"; Coro: "Steiniget ihn"
Stoning					
10. Rec.: "Und sie steinigten ihn"; Choral: "Dir, Herr, will ich mich ergeben"	10. Rec.: "Und sie steinigten ihn"; Choral: "Dir, Herr, will ich mich ergeben"		10. Rec.: "Und sie steinigten ihn"; Choral: "Dir, Herr, will ich mich ergeben"	10. Rec.: "Und sie steinigten ihn"; Choral: "Dir, Herr, will ich mich ergeben"	9. Rec.: "Und sie steinigten ihn"; Choral: "Dir, Herr, will ich mich ergeben"
11. Der du die Menschen	11. Der du die Menschen		11. Der du die Menschen	11. Der du die Menschen	

Source: Sposato, Jeffrey, *Mendelssohn's Theological Evolution: A Study of Textual Choice and Change in the Composer's Sacred Works.*

Figure 4.2. MN53, p. 49.

Interestingly enough, however, MN53 contains one revision that did not get transferred into MN55 or its clean copy (PS-NYPL), even though it appears in the revised form in the printed program. Mendelssohn changed the words of the opening of the recitative from "Da bewegten sie das Volk" to the shorter and more direct "Und bewegten das Volk." Mendelssohn might have made this change after he had already sent off MN55 to be copied and then either forgot or did not think this change was important enough to change in the piano-vocal score.

The chorus "Dieser Mensch hört nicht auf" also shows many layers of revisions, as can be seen in Table 4.6.

Table 4.6. Revision Stages of "Dieser Mensch hört nicht auf"

1. MN53I	52-58a	+	[59-62]	+	63-68a
2. MN53II	52-58b	+	[59-62]	+	63-68b
3. MN55I	22-28a				
4. MN55II	22-28b				
5. MN53III	52-58b	+	59-62a	+	63-68b
6. MN53IV	52-58c	+	59-62b	+	63-68c
MN55III	22-28c				
7. PS-NYPL					
8. Simrock					

All the revisions from MN53I to MN53II are made in order to increase clarity. In the vocal parts these changes either are redistributions of syllables or simplifications or omissions of vocal parts (see Figure 4.3). Each of those revisions serves the purpose of bringing out the text better. The revisions in the orchestra serve the same purpose; several times Mendelssohn decided to drop a line in the brass by an octave or to eliminate it completely.

The revisions from MN55I to MN55II are mainly structural. Mendelssohn excised three measures and then one further measure to make the revised section more concise and less repetitive (see Examples 4.7a and b). The last revision stage in MN53 and MN55 shows only few minor changes concerning the voicing of chords.

The clean piano-vocal score copy (PS-NYPL) shows a few minor additions. All are either more dynamic markings or are accent marks.

The printed Simrock version also does not have many corrections beyond MN53IV and MN55III. All of them are minor voice-leading changes that do not affect the perception of the movement.

Figure 4.3. MN53, p. 55.

Example 4.7a. MN55I, "Dieser Mensch hört nicht auf"

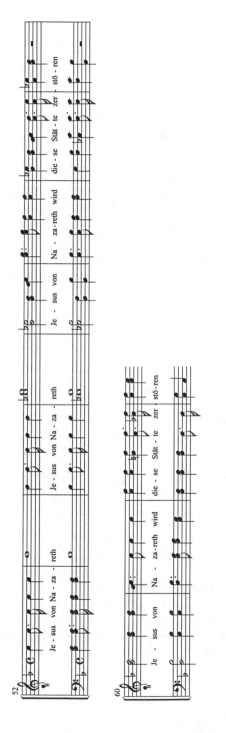

Example 4.7b. MN55II, "Dieser Mensch hört nicht auf"

Trial

The second part of the scene, the trial, consists of two numbers, a recitative with an interjected turba choir and an aria. The recitative and chorus textually form the longest number in the first part of the oratorio. The length of the text and its content, Stephen's sermon—a monologue, make this movement problematic because of its potential to stall the dramatic flow of the scene. The revisions of this number clearly illustrate Mendelssohn's struggle with the issue of keeping the drama going in this long monologue. Table 4.7 shows the revision stages of these two numbers.

Table 4.7. Revision Stages of "Und sie sahen auf ihn alle"

1. MN53I	69-70a	+	[71-x]			
2. MN53II	69-70b	+	[71-x]			
3. MN55I	29-33a					
4. MN55II	29-33b					
5. PS-NYPL						
6. MN53III	69-70c	+	71-74	+	[75-x]	
7. MN53IV	69-70c	+	71-74	+	75-76	
8. Simrock						

Table 4.7 shows that MN53 consists of three discrete physical sections (69-70, 71-74, 75-76). Although the two later sections show no revisions, the first section has signs of heavy revisions; these include crossed-out measures and a heavily revised vocal line, as well as corrections in the instrumental parts (see Figure 4.4). The last several measures are crossed out; the revision of these measures can be seen in the second, newer section (71-74). A comparison of these crossed-out measures with the revised version of MN53III reveals Mendelssohn's concern in his revisions to keep the scene dramatic throughout this long recitative. Piano reductions of these passages in Examples 4.8a and b show the drastic revisions, turning a simple, straight-forward recitative into a much more intense arioso.

Figure 4.4. MN53, p. 69.

The cross-outs in MN53 show that MN55 falls in between MN53II and MN53III in terms of the revision process. For the first time there are heavy revisions in MN55 that predate MN53. Interestingly, with the beginning of the recitative the paper in MN55 changes to type B. The

Example. 4.8a. MN53II, "Und sie sahen auf ihn alle" I

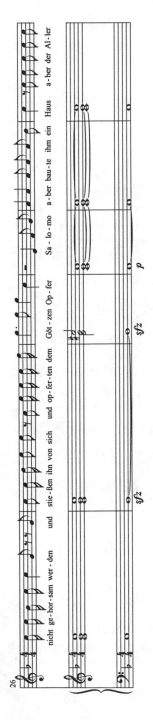

Example 4.8b. MN53III, "Und sie sahen auf ihn alle" I

revisions made in MN55 are not as thorough as the example, since Mendelssohn already had made this type of revision earlier. Nevertheless, they also serve the same purpose of heightening the intensity level, albeit on a much smaller scale. Twice Mendelssohn cut measures that contained repetition, thereby guaranteeing a quicker tempo of the unfolding story. In measure 54 of the recitative he changed a less effective stepwise ascent into a more expressive leap on the words "und sie getödtet" (see Examples 4.9a and b).

Example 4.9a. MN55I, "Und sie sahen auf ihn alle," II

Example 4.9b. MN55II, "Und sie sahen auf ihn alle," II

Other revisions from MN55II to MN53III include the cutting of text. Mendelssohn changed "welches ihr nun Verräther und Mörder geworden seid" to the shorter "dessen Mörder ihr geworden seid." This revision is interesting for another reason. Both MN55II and PS-NYPL still use the longer text, while the program of the first performance already uses the shortened text. This seems to indicate that PS-NYPL does not represent the first performance version; rather, it predates it, as does MN55.

Another textual cut was made in the revision from MN53IV to the printed version (Simrock). Mendelssohn cut out "und sie getödtet" from "Welche Propheten haben eure Väter nicht verfolgt und sie getödtet, die. . . ." Again, Mendelssohn wanted to speed up the action by keeping the text short and concise. All of the other revisions from MN53IV to the Simrock version appear in the vocal part and are fairly small; they are similar melodic adjustments to the one discussed earlier in MN55.

The revision process of the ensuing aria of Stephen, "Jerusalem," is the same as it was toward the end of the recitative. MN53 is fairly clean, because it only shows one layer of revisions. The printed Sim-rock version is identical to the revised version of MN53, but MN55 and, surprisingly, PS-NYPL, contain several layers of revision. Most of the revisions are focused on the second half of the A section of this short da capo aria. Mendelssohn changed the text from "und steinigest" to "die du steinigest," which makes it a parallel construction to "die du tödtest." By doing so he was able to intensify the phrase more effec-tively, also using the same motivic material for both phrases. It is very important to note that PS-NYPL shows corrections in Mendelssohn's own hand, which establishes PS-NYPL as a copy that represents revi-sion stages intertwined with MN53 and MN55.

The Stoning of Stephen

The first number of this last part of the scene, a recitative and a chorus, shows few revisions. This is not surprising, since they are written mostly on type B paper. Ms. 1092, a leaf of an earlier version of "Steiniget ihn" is paper of type A, confirming that MN53 contains a revised version of this chorus. The ensuing number, a recitative and a chorale show even fewer revisions; Table 4.8 shows the stages of revi-sions of both numbers.

Table 4.8 Revision Stages of "Und sie stürmten/Steiniget ihn" and "Und sie steinigten ihn/Dir Herr will ich"

1. Ms. 1092 (fragment of "Steiniget ihn")
2. MN55ac
3. MN55pc
PS-NYPL
MN53
4. Simrock

Surprisingly, the section contained on the leaf with the fragment of "Steiniget ihn" is very close to the later versions, which means that the pages surrounding this leaf must have been the reason for the replace-ment of the earlier version. Few revisions are found in any of the movements of this in MN55. Most of them concern voicing; several times a lower vocal part drops an octave, at other times chordal tones are redistributed. Mendelssohn cut out one measure with the repeated text "steiniget ihn," which reduced the number of repetitions of the text from four to three. Two more textual cuts were made in individual voices where text is repeated unnecessarily. Only two revisions were made in the printed version from MN53. Both are orchestral changes. The first change cut the doubling of the bass line by the trombones (mm. 12-13). The second revision is found in the timpani, adding a one-measure roll and the doubling of the rhythm in the strings over the next two measures (mm. 47-49).

While the printed version ends with the chorale, MN53 and all the earlier versions contain an aria here, "Der du die Menschen." The text for this aria is taken from Psalm 90:3-6; Schubring, in his first draft from 23 January 1833, suggested Psalm 90:2, 5, 12-13, with the note that Mendelssohn might be able to pick out more fitting verses from Psalm 90.[5] The reasons for Mendelssohn's omission of the aria are textual rather than musical. Since the preceding chorale already supplies a reflective insertion into the drama, it seems redundant to add a lyrical aria here. Furthermore, since the opening movements closed with a chorale, it seems more fitting that the next major section of the oratorio should once again close with a chorale.

MN53 and MN55 show several revisions; PS-NYPL contains a clean copy of the revised MN55 version, and, like the previous movements, MN55 preceded MN53. The revisions in both manuscripts are minor except for two passages. Mendelssohn revised these passages several times. The latest stage found in MN53 shows a shortened and arguably more concise version than the earlier versions of MN55 and PS-NYPL. The introduction shows that Mendelssohn was concerned with clarity and concision. Mendelssohn shortened the introduction twice, once in the initial version of MN53 (MN53ac) and then again in MN53pc.

Saul's Persecution of the Christians

Overview

The second scene of *Paulus* is fairly short. Even though this scene contains Stephen's burial, its main purpose is to introduce Saul and portray him as the enemy and persecutor of Christians such as Stephen. Primarily, the second scene is intended to set up the climax of the first part, Saul's conversion (see Table 4.9).

In the earliest drafts Mendelssohn did not use the portrayal of Saul, before his conversion, as a separate scene. At some point Saul became part of the crowd at the stoning of Stephen. In his third draft (c. 27, pp. 28r-30v) Mendelssohn started to portray Saul as persecutor immediately following the stoning scene. Mendelssohn's portrayal of Saul as the persecutor is fairly short and unfocused, however; the mention of Saul's activities against the Christians was part of a long recitative that included Stephen's sermon and stoning. After the recitative follows Saul's *Rachearie*, "Vertilge sie." Starting with MN53 Mendelssohn made the portrayal of Saul as the hateful and brutal persecutor a separate scene. This change sets up more effectively Saul's conversion as the climax of part 1.

Recitatives

The most obvious revisions in this section of the oratorio are found in the recitatives. The text distribution of the recitatives of MN53 and MN55/PS-NYPL is different from that of the published version (see Examples 4.10a and b). In MN53 and MN55/PS-NYPL Acts 8:2, "Es beschickten aber. . ." is used for the text of the first recitative; the text for the second recitative is from the previous chapter, 7:57, "Und die Zeugen hatten abgelegt"; the text of the last recitative then is again taken from the passage of the first recitative, Acts 8:3, "Und Paulus zerstörte die Gemeinde." The fact that Mendelssohn used Bible passages here out of their chronological order demonstrates that the composer created this separate scene for dramatic effect: Mendelssohn compensated for his chronological rearrangement through the change of the text from "Und die Zeugen legten ab ihre Kleider" to "Und die Zeugen hatten abgelegt ihre Kleider." In the Simrock version Mendelssohn restored the texts of the recitatives to the chronological order of Acts.

The recitative "Es beschickten aber" only shows one revision in MN53. Mendelssohn added this short recitative at a later date by squeezing it onto the last page of the previous movement. His only revision, which was made immediately after he wrote the first measure, changes the part from tenor, as it was scored in MN55 and PS-NYPL, to soprano. "Tenore" is crossed out and "Soprano" is written underneath it; the clef is changed from soprano to tenor, and the accidentals

Table 4.9 Sources of Part 1, Scene 2

Libretto sources

FMB—MDM c.42	Schubring—d. 30, no. 214	Marx—d. 53, no. 88	FMB—d.30, no. 211; Schubring's comments	FMB—c. 27, p. 28r-30v
"Gott mache sie wie einen Wirbel, wie Stoppeln" "Und die Zeugen legten" "...Saulus aber zustörte die Gemeinde..."	10. Rec.: "Und sie stießen ihn" 11. Saulus: "Gott mache sie wie einen Wirbel, wie Stoppeln" p.p.	Rec.: "Saulus aber schnaubte" Doppelchor mit Solo: "Sie sind nieder-gestürzt" Saulus: "Wie lange wollt ihr" Chor 1: "Der Herr wird sie", Chor 2: "Wenn ich rufe zu dir" Rec.: "Und ging zum Hohenpriester" Arie: "Wer ist, der so fehlet"	[Rec.:] "Und die Zeugen legten" Arie: "Gott mache sie wie einen Wirbel, wie Stoppeln" [Rec.:] "Es bestellten aber" [Chorus:] Psalm 90 [Chorale:] "Jesus meine Zuversicht"	[Rec.:] "Paulus aber hatte Wohlgefallen" Aria: "Gott mache sie wie Stoppeln"

Musical sources

MN19	MN28	MN55	PS-NYPL	MN53	Program of premier	Simrock	Other sources
page of full score and continuity draft of "Vertilge sie"	13. Chor: "Herr Gott, des die Rache ist "	12. Rec.: "Es beschickten aber" 13. Chor: "Siehe, wir preisen selig" 14. Rec.: "Und die Zeugen"/["Vertilge Zeugen"/Aria "Vertilge sie" is cut] 15. Rec.: "Und Saulus zerstörte" instead of 16., FMB writes: "hier folgt eine Arie"	12. Rec.: "Es beschickten aber" 13. [9.] Chor: "Siehe, wir preisen selig" 14. Rec.: "Und die Zeugen"/Aria "Vertilge sie" 15. Rec.: "Und Saulus zerstörte"	12. Rec.: "Es beschickten aber" 13. Chor: "Siehe, wir preisen selig" 14. Rec.: "Und die Zeugen"/Aria "Vertilge sie" 15. Rec.: "Und Saulus zerstörte" 16. Arioso: "Doch der Herr vergißt"	12. Rec.: "Es beschickten aber" 13. Chor: "Siehe, wir preisen selig" 14. Rec.: "Und die Zeugen"/Aria "Vertilge sie" 15. Rec.: "Und Saulus zerstörte" 16. Arioso: "Doch der Herr vergißt"	10. Rec.: "Und die Zeugen" 11. Chor: "Siehe, wir preisen selig" 12. Rec.: "Saulus aber zerstörte"/Aria "Vertilge sie" 13. Rec.: "Und zog mit einer Schar" 13. (cont.) Aria: "Doch der Herr vergißt"	16. Aria: "Doch der Herr er leitet" (Mus. ms. 1445b)

Source: Sposato, Jeffrey, *Mendelssohn's Theological Evolution: A Study of Textual Choice and Change in the Composer's Sacred Works.*

Example 4.10a. Recitative Texts of Part 1, Scene 2 in MN53/MN55/PS-NYPL

No. 12

Es beschickten aber Stephanum gottesfürchtige Männer, und hielten große Klage über ihn (Acts 8:2)

No. 14

Und die Zeugen hatten abgelegt ihre Kleider, zu den Füßen eines Jünglings, der hieß Saulus (Acts 7:57), der hatte Wohlgefallen an seinem Tode (Acts 8:1) und sprach:

No. 15

Und Saulus zerstörte die Gemeinde (Acts 8:3), und schnaubte noch mit Drohen und Morden wider die Jünger des Herrns (Acts 9:1). Und zog mit einer Schar gen Damascus und hatte Macht und Befehl von den Hohenpriestern, Männer und Weiber gebunden zu führen gen Jerusalem (Acts 9:2).

Example 4.10b. Recitative Texts of Part 1, Scene 2 in Simrock

No. 9

Und die Zeugen legten ab ihre Kleider zu den Füßen eines Jünglings der hieß Saulus (Acts 7:57); der hatte Wohlgefallen an seinem Tode (Acts 8:1a). Es beschickten aber Stephanum gottesfürchtige Männer und hielten eine große Klage über ihn (Acts 8:2).

No. 11

Saulus aber zerstörte die Gemeinde (Acts 8:3), und wütete mit Drohen und Morden wider die Jünger (Acts 9:1) und lästerte sie und sprach:

and the notes of the first measure are adjusted accordingly (see Figure 4.5). This change seems odd. The preceding aria is for soprano; one would expect a different soloist, namely the tenor, to sing the immediately ensuing recitative, which also seems to have been Mendelssohn's first thought.

A look at the other two recitatives in the manuscripts only complicates the matter. In both cases Mendelssohn reassigned the vocal parts. In the second recitative, "Und die Zeugen hatten abgelegt," immediately after writing "Soprano" into the score Mendelssohn changed it to "Tenore." This revision seems arbitrary, since there seems to be no strong reason for either soloist. The third recitative, "Und Saulus zerstörte die Gemeinde," is rewritten in MN55 to make a change from alto to soprano possible. This change can be explained by the ensuing arioso, which was written for alto voice; to avoid back-to-back recitative and aria movements for the same soloist, Mendelssohn rewrote the recitative for soprano voice. This revision makes his earlier change in the

Figure 4.5. MN53, p. 94.

manuscript, which actually assigns two consecutive movements to the same soloist, seem inconsistent.

The second recitative, "Und die Zeugen hatten abgelegt," does not have any corrections in either of the manuscript sources other than the redistribution of soloists in MN53. The third recitative, "Und Saulus zerstörte die Gemeinde," however, was heavily revised. In changing the voice part from alto in MN53 to soprano in MN55 Mendelssohn was forced to rewrite the recitative to fit the higher vocal part. Because Mendelssohn kept the harmonic structure and key of MN53, however, he only had to rewrite the vocal part (see Examples 4.11a and b).

Example 4.11a. MN53, "Und Paulus zerstörte die Gemeinde"

Example 4.11b. MN 55, "Und Paulus zerstörte die Gemeinde"

Choruses

The revision stages of the chorus "Siehe, wir preisen selig" are shown in Table 4.10.

Table 4.10. Revision Stages of "Siehe, wir preisen selig"

1. MN53ac
2. N53pc
3. MN55ac
4. MN55pc/PS-NYPL
5. Simrock

MN53 shows the heaviest revisions, but Mendelssohn did not make any structural changes in this manuscript, and the pitch changes are limited to voicing and register. In the instrumental parts he added horns at the bottom of the score to give added harmonic support. All of the other revisions are textual. Most of them redistribute syllables. Mendelssohn's aim, as we have seen before, was to increase clarity. Most textual revisions cut out repetitions through the use of longer melismas, making the polyphonic texture sound less agitated and busy (see Figure 4.6). In this way Mendelssohn emphasized the lyrical aspect of the text. The most surprising change, however, is the introduction of new text without any musical changes. Since the original text was quite a short one for a whole movement, one would expect that the introduction of additional text should warrant major musical changes. Mendelssohn did not change the music; rather, he merely crossed out the existing text, which was just another text repetition, and wrote the new text underneath it. This new text appears for the first time here. Although both texts are based on Bible verses and are related in content, they are not grouped together in the Bible. The old text is based on James 1:12, the new text on 2 Corinthians 4:10-11. The choice of new text must have been studied carefully, for no syllabic adjustments were necessary (see Example 4.12). Because Mendelssohn introduced this new text at the contrasting section of the movement, this textual revision works quite well.

Mendelssohn added a new interpretive dimension through the addition of the text. Up to that point the emphasis was on the martyrdom of Stephen for his Christian belief. The new text, however, points out the reward for uncompromising Christian living: eternal life. The addition of the new text here shows a shift from mere drama to a more complete theological interpretation of the narration and its application to all Christians.

Figure 4.6. MN53, p. 97.

Example 4.12. Text of "Siehe, wir preisen selig"

>   >   >   >   >

Sie- he   wir prei-sen   se- lig,   die er- dul-ded ha-ben!

>   >   >   >   >

Denn ob der Leib gleich   stirbt, doch wird die   See-le   le-ben.

MN55 shows only five minor revisions in all; PS-NYPL is a clean copy of MN55pc. The Simrock edition does not contain any further revisions.

The chorus "Herr Gott, deß die Rache ist, erscheine" is a rejected movement that only appears in MN28. While the text for this chorus does not appear in any of the libretto drafts, it is safe to assume that this chorus was originally written as part of this scene. The chorus is numbered "No. 13," and the text fits the context of this scene. "Herr Gott, deß die Rache ist, erscheine" was written for bass solo and chorus; the bass solo presumably was to represent Saul. While Kurzhals-Reuter assumes that "Herr Gott, deß die Rache ist erscheine" was replaced by "Vertilge sie,"[6] it seems more plausible that Mendelssohn composed the aria and the chorus to be side by side. Even the early libretto stages include a type of *Rachearie*, and, as Michael Cooper has pointed out, it is hard to imagine that Mendelssohn did not include a *Rachearie* in his earlier drafts.[7]

Arias

The first of the two arias in this section of the oratorio, "Vertilge sie," is the most heavily revised movement in this scene. Table 4.11 shows the revision stages of the aria.

Table 4.11. Revision Stages of "Vertilge sie"

1. MN19, p. 5 (incomplete)
2. MN19, p. 11 (continuity draft)
3. MN55ac
4. MN55pc
PS-NYPL
5. MN53ac
6. MN53pc
Simrock

Stages 1 and 2, found in MN19, are only drafts of the aria. Page 5 of MN19 (stage 1) contains two systems of music initially intended as full score. Since this page does not contain the beginning of the movement, the instrumentation is not specified other than by the clef and key signature. It is scored for orchestra and solo bass voice. Only the vocal part and bass line, however, were used. The rest of the page was used later for a continuity draft of "Mache dich auf, werde Licht." The text is the same as that of some of the earlier libretto draft, suggesting that this page stems from an early attempt to set the suggested aria text to music. The music is unrelated to the later continuity draft and versions. Stage 2 is a continuity draft that is motivically related to the complete versions (page 11 of MN19). Framing the aria are two recitatives also unrelated to later versions.[8] Stages 3 through 6 are complete drafts of the aria "Vertilge sie." Stages 3 and 5 are drastically different versions of the aria, however, with stages 4 and 6 representing revisions of those different versions. The version of MN55ac is 77 measures longer than the MN53ac version. During the revision process leading to the MN53 version Mendelssohn made more severe cuts. Both versions use ternary form, but the lengths of the respective sections within each version differ greatly (see Table 4.12).

Table 4.12. Proportional Makeup of "Vertilge sie"

	MN55ac	MN53ac
Section A	99 mm./50.77%	38 mm./32.2%
Section B	65 mm./33.33%	35 mm./29.66%
Section A	31 mm./15.9%	45 mm./38.14%

The most obvious difference is that the sections of MN53ac are much closer to equal length than were those in MN55ac.

A comparison of the A sections explains the differing lengths found in MN55ac and MN53ac. The earlier, longer version, after stating the text once, modulates to the dominant key, F-sharp minor; the text is repeated to music with developmental character. The revised, shorter version of MN53 states the text once, repeats only the first line of text, and modulates to F-sharp minor, which becomes the key of the B section. The main motivic material is retained from the earlier version.

The B sections differ musically as well as textually. The earlier version of MN55 modulates to the contrast key of G major and its relative key, E minor. The text as well as the music make for the strong contrast to the A section. The mood switches surprisingly from hate

and vengeance to either self-doubt or a display of false righteousness.
Mendelssohn used Psalm 139:23, "Search me, O God, and know my
heart; Try me and know my anxious thoughts."[9] It quickly becomes
clear that Saul is quoting it out of a false self-righteousness, for the text
does not continue to the next verse of the Psalm, "And see if there be
any hurtful way in me, And lead me in the everlasting way" (Psalm
139:24). Rather, he uses parts of the preceding verses, "I hate them
with utmost hatred" (Psalm 139:22), "Do I not hate those who hate
Thee, O Lord" (Psalm 139:21). In the revised version of MN53 Mendelssohn did not use such contrasting material either in the music or in
the text. The words "Laß deinen Zorn sie treffen, verstummen müssen
sie" echo the hatred of the A section; the music is related to that of the
A section, it stays in the closely related key of F-sharp minor.

The closing A' sections have also different functions in the two
versions. In the longer, earlier version A' becomes a shortened coda-
like section using material from the opening section. The later version
balances out the two previous sections, recapitulating all the themes.

The revisions within MN55 already show Mendelssohn's attempts
to make the aria more concise; measures are cut and phrases are shortened. The revisions found in MN53 are much less severe; most of them
are changes in the vocal parts, smoothing out leaps to produce more
stepwise lines. There are some revisions in the instrumental parts as
well; all of these make for a lighter orchestration.

The arioso "Doch der Herr vergißt der Seinen nicht" is only found
in MN53 and the Simrock version. In MN55 Mendelssohn wrote underneath "No. 15," which refers to the third recitative, "Hier folgt eine
Arie." The next movement is no. 17, a recitative and chorus. PS-NYPL
not only does not contain this aria, it continues with the recitative and
chorus as no. 16, which throws off the numbering of PS-NYPL from
this point on. Obviously Mendelssohn decided fairly late in the revision
process to insert this arioso.

Before Mendelssohn settled on this arioso, he wrote another aria to
be inserted here, "Doch derr Herr er leitet die Irrenden recht." The only
extant autograph of this aria is a piano vocal written on a single leaf of
type B paper (Mus. ms. 1445b). The text is taken from Psalm 25 and
focuses on God's sovereignty in guiding the sinner towards grace; the
text in this context applies to Saul's upcoming conversion. The text of
the arioso, "Doch der Herr vergißt der Seinen nicht," is not based on a
Bible passage, and its focus is not on Saul but rather on God's promise
to protect his suffering church. This textual revision deserves attention,
as it places Saul's conversion in the larger context of the history of the
early church.

The revisions of the arioso "Doch der Herr vergißt der Seinen nicht" are minor. The version contained in MN53 and the published version are fairly close. Mendelssohn only cut one measure, the penultimate measure of the MN53 version, which had merely prolonged the final cadence. Otherwise the revisions are all rhythmic adjustments in the vocal line.

Saul's Conversion

Overview

The third scene of the oratorio is the centerpiece of the first part. It is divided into two sections: Jesus' appearance to Saul and Saul's response of repentance and belief. Table 4.13 shows the evolution of this scene.

Jesus' Appearance to Saul

This section is in many ways the climax of part 1, even though it is not the end of the first part of the oratorio. Saul, the persecutor of the Christians, is knocked to the ground and blinded by Jesus, whom Saul considered a dead lunatic. Saul's life turns on this event—the hater of Christians will become their foremost teacher, and the persecutor will become one of the persecuted. Mendelssohn presumably was well aware of the importance of this section of the oratorio when he wrote to Schubring about it: "Immediately after the Lord's words to St. Paul on his conversion I have introduced a great chorus, 'Arise, arise and shine' (Isaiah lx. 1, 2), and this I, as yet, consider the best movement of the first part."[10] Mendelssohn's third draft (c. 27, pp. 28r-30v) has the words for this chorus, "Mache dich auf, werde Licht" added on the right half of the page, which he left empty for such text revisions. Starting with MN53 Mendelssohn added the chorale "Wachet auf! ruft uns die Stimme." This underlines even more the importance of this section, since the chorale tune is also the basis of the overture.[11]

Mendelssohn could have approached Saul's conversion quite differently. He could have emphasized Saul's response of faith as the key element of his salvation. Only a single aria, "Gott, sei mir gnädig," expressed Paul's response of faith, while God's offer of salvation is expressed in the chorus "Mache dich auf, werde Licht," as well as in the

Table 4.13. Sources of Part 1, Scene 3

		Libretto sources		
FMB—MDM c.42	Fürst—d. 53, no. 87; d. 30, no. 211	Marx—d. 53, no. 88	FMB—d.30, no. 211; Schubring's comments	FMB—c. 27, p. 28r-30v
		Jesus' appearance to Paul		
Saul zieht nach Damascus (Acts 8:1, 3; 9:1-2)	[Rec.:] "Saulus aber schnaubte"\	Rec.: "Und da er auf dem Wege war"	[Rec.:] "Und da er auf dem Wege war"	[Rec.:] "Und da er auf dem Wege war"
Die Erscheinung (Acts 9:3-9)	Der Herr: "Saul, Saul"	Die Stimme: "Saul, Saul"		Chor: "Mache dich auf, werde Licht"
				Arie: "Deine Sonne wird nicht"
	Saulus: "Herr, wer bist du"	[Saulus:] "Herr, wer bist du"		
	Der Herr: "Ich bin Jesus"	Die Stimme: "Ich bin Jesus"		
	Saulus: "Herr, was willst du"	[Saulus:] "Herr, was willst du"		
	Der Herr: "Stehe auf"	Die Stimme: "Stehe auf"		
		Chor mit Solo: "Fürchte dich nicht"		
		Rec.: "Die Männer aber"		
		Chor: "Was will das werden?"		
		Paul's response of repentance		
		Rec.: "Saulus aber richtete"		[Rec.:] "Die Männer aber"
		Arie mit Chor (Altst., nicht Paulus): "Verwirf mich nicht"		Solo: "Schaffe in mir Gott"
				[?:] "Herr thue meine Lippen auf"

Continued on next page

(Table 4.13—*Continued*)

		Musical sources		
MN55ac/MN53ac	MN55pc/MN53pc	PS—NYPL	Program of premier	Simrock
		Jesus' appearance to Paul		
No. 14 Rec.: "Und als er auf dem Wege war"; Chor: "Saul, Saul"; Rec.: "Er aber sprach"; Chor: "Ich bin Jesus"; Rec.: "Und er sprach"; Chor: "Stehe auf"	No. 17 Rec.: "Und als er auf dem Wege war"; Chor: "Saul, Saul"; Rec.: "Er aber sprach"; Chor: "Ich bin Jesus"; Rec.: "Und er sprach"; Chor: "Stehe auf"	No. 16 Rec.: "Und als er auf dem Wege war"; Chor: "Saul, Saul"; Rec.: "Er aber sprach"; Chor: "Ich bin Jesus"; Rec.: "Und er sprach"; Chor: "Stehe auf"	Nr. 17 Rec.: "Und als er auf dem Wege war"; Chor: "Saul, Saul"; Rec.: "Er aber sprach"; Chor: "Ich bin Jesus"; Rec.: "Und er sprach"; Chor: "Stehe auf"	14. Rec.: "Und als er auf dem Wege war"; Chor: "Saul, Saul"; Rec.: "Er aber sprach"; Chor: "Ich bin Jesus"; Rec.: "Und er sprach"; Chor: "Stehe auf"
No. 15 Chor: "Mache dich auf, werde Licht!"	No. 18 Chor: "Mache dich auf, werde Licht!"	No. 17 Chor: "Mache dich auf, werde Licht!"	Nr. 18 Chor: "Mache dich auf, werde Licht!"	15. Chorus: "Mache dich auf, werde Licht!"
No. 16 Choral "Wachet auf! ruft uns die Stimme"	No. 19 Choral "Wachet auf! ruft uns die Stimme"	No. 18 Choral "Wachet auf! ruft uns die Stimme"	Nr. 19 Choral "Wachet auf! ruft uns die Stimme"	16. Choral "Wachet auf! ruft uns die Stimme"
		Paul's response of repentance		
No. 17 Rec.: "Die Männer aber"	No. 20 Rec.: "Die Männer aber"	No. 19 Rec.: "Die Männer aber"	Nr. 20 Rec.: "Die Männer aber"	17. Rec.: "Die Männer aber"
No. 18 Aria: "Gott, sei mir gnädig"	No. 21 Aria: "Gott, sei mir gnädig"	No. 20 Aria: "Gott, sei mir gnädig"	Nr. 21 Aria: "Gott, sei mir gnädig"	18. Aria: "Gott, sei mir gnädig"

Source. Sposato, Jeffrey, *Mendelssohn's Theological Evolution: A Study of Textual Choice and Change in the Composer's Sacred Works.*

ensuing chorale, "Wachet auf! ruft uns die Stimme." It is God's action, reaching down to Saul out of mercy, that is interpreted as the main factor of Saul's salvation. Mendelssohn's portrayal in Saul's salvation as a gift of grace that is initiated by God rather than the sinner is based on a Lutheran view of salvation.

Recitative

The recitative contains the narration for this scene; it is taken directly from Acts and was a part of every libretto draft. The revision stages of "Und als er auf dem Wege war" are shown in Table 4.14.

Table 4.14. Revision Stages of "Und als er auf dem Wege war"

1. MN53I	[x-120]	+	121-122ac
2. MN53II	[x-120]	+	121-122pc
3. MN55I	57-58ac		
4. MN55II	57-58pc		
5. PS-NYPL			
6. MN53III	117-120ac	+	121-122pc
7. MN53IV	117-122pc		
8. Simrock			

The last two pages (121-122) are all that is extant of the earliest musical setting of this recitative (see stage 1 in Table 4.14). Mendelssohn was able to use this single page because he did not need to make many corrections. Only the first three measures are considerably revised and are thus crossed out; the folio inserted later is laid out in such a way as to line up with the older page.

MN55I contains the earliest available version of the opening. In the second measure of the recitative, Mendelssohn changed the words from "[Und als er auf dem Wege war,] die Männer und Weiber gebunden führte" to "und nahe zu Damaskus kam." The crossed-out words were not taken from Acts; Saul was on his way to arrest Christians, but he had not arrested anybody yet. This rejected attempt suggests that Mendelssohn possibly wanted to add more interest to Saul's conversion through the placement of arrested Christians in that scene. Mendelssohn did not take that idea very far, however, as the corrections suggest. In this case, then, Mendelssohn chose the more accurate story line over a more sensational setting.

Besides this rejected attempt to add interest to the scene by changing the story line, the other revisions focus on musical means to heighten the intensity of this recitative. A comparison of the vocal lines of the opening in MN55I and the published Simrock version provides a demonstration (see Examples 4.13a and b). All the changes help bring out the important words ("plötzlich" and "Stimme") and phrases ("die sprach zu ihm").

Example 4.13a. MN55I, "Und als er auf dem Wege war"

Example 4.13b. Simrock, "Und als er auf dem Wege war"

The most effective revision in the dramatic effect of this recitative, however, was not made until after the first performance in Düsseldorf. The Simrock edition has the words of Saul sung by a different soloist, the bass (the voice part always used for Saul), while the rest of the recitative is still sung by the tenor. This revision adds a new dimension to the performance of the work, because the representation of the action becomes more realistic.

Chorus

"Mache dich auf" is the longest chorus of the oratorio; it is also one of the most complex movements in *Paulus*. Starting with the versions in MN53, it did not undergo the sort of extensive revisions of form or counterpoint that some of the other more complex movements did. Table 4.15 shows the revision stages of this chorus.

Table 4.15. Revision Stages of "Mache dich auf"

1. MN19 6-5			
2. MN53I123-124ac	+	[125-x]	
3. MN53II	123-124pc	+	[125-x]
4. MN53III	123-124pc	+	125-143I
5. MN53IV	123-124pc	+	124-143II
MN55ac			
6. MN53V	123-124pc	+	124-143III
MN55pc			
PS-NYPL			
7. Simrock			

MN19 contains a continuity draft of the chorus. While the main motivic material is already found in this draft, this source gives only an outline of this long and complex movement. The sections are shorter and unfocused, simply capturing the basic idea and direction of this movement.[12]

The lack of evidence of substantial revisions in the complete versions can be explained by the fact that there was at least one earlier complete draft of the movement, of which we only have the first two pages (MN53, pp. 123-124). These two pages complete the last bifolio of the preceding recitative. This bifolio survives from an earlier version written on the earlier used paper type C, while the rest of the movement is written on paper type B; only complete bifolios are used, which might suggest that Mendelssohn already had a rigorous revision process behind him at this stage.

The only revisions found on these first two pages are in the woodwinds and horns. The entrance of the horns is moved back two measures; the clarinets and bassoons stay in the lower register rather than moving up. This change delays the crescendo, making its conclusion more powerful. The revisions in the instrumental parts on the later-inserted pages of MN53 are all cross-outs of sustained notes, which make a more transparent texture.

The changes to the vocal parts in MN53 are small but numerous. Many of them adjust syllables, either to make them fit better with the music or to synchronize different parts better with each other (see Figure 4.7). Pitch changes mostly are made to increase clarity; a few times a vocal part is dropped out or slowed down because of an entrance in one of the other parts (see Figure 4.8). The register of the sopranos is dropped several times from high to low, spacing the more climactic higher sections further apart over the course of the movement.

The vocal parts of MN55I are identical with those of MN53IV. After writing out the piano reduction in MN55, Mendelssohn revised the movement once again; both MN53 and MN55 share several revisions in the vocal parts, all of which serve the same purposes described above. PS-NYPL is a clean copy of MN55II. The Simrock edition is almost identical with MN53V. The few instrumental changes once more lighten the instrumental texture; there are in all five minute adjustments of syllable placement in the vocal lines.

Chorale

The chorale "Wachet auf! ruft uns die Stimme" is treated differently from the previous two chorales. In the first two chorales the instruments merely double the vocal four-part setting, in the third chorale the instrumental parts are used at times independently. The addition of these independent instrumental parts clearly underscores the dramatic moment in the oratorio. There are only three revision stages of the cho-

Figure 4.7. MN53, p. 130.

rale (see Table 4.16). The first set of revisions is not as significant as the second set. Mendelssohn cut out single measures twice at fermatas, and he made minor voice changes. The later revisions, however, are more drastic. The repetition of the first part of the hymn is taken out, cutting a section of the original hymn text. Since the hymn text is co-

Figure 4.8. MN53, p. 134.

herent without the omitted text, Mendelssohn saw the shortening of the chorale as more important than the use of the complete text. Besides shortening the chorale, the composer also revised the harmonization considerably (see Examples 4.14a and b). The changes in harmonization seem to have been done due to two main reasons: (1) to have a smoother bass line (compare mm. 7-19 of both versions), and (2) to make the harmonic progressions more colorful (compare harmonic progressions of mm. 1-2).

Table 4.16. Revision Stages of "Wachet auf!"

1. MN53I
2. MN53II
MN55I
3. MN53III
MN55II
PS-NYPL
Simrock

Saul's Response

The second part of the conversion scene consists only of a recitative, describing a disoriented Saul being led to Damascus, and an aria, expressing Saul's realization of his sinfulness. Appropriately, Mendelssohn used verses from Psalm 51, which express King David's recognition of his guilt after being confronted about it by a prophet. The first time Psalm 51 appeared in the course of the oratorio's development was in Mendelssohn's third draft, c. 27, pp. 28r-30v. Fürst also quoted from Psalm 51 in his suggestions, albeit in a different context. This might have drawn Mendelssohn's attention to Psalm 51 and the relationship of its content to this scene.

Recitative

The revision stages of this short recitative are simple and straightforward. Only MN53 shows any corrections written into the manuscripts. Mendelssohn delayed a chord change by half a measure, from the middle of the bar to the next measure; toward the end he revoiced a chord for dramatic purposes, creating a large leap in the first violins at the words "und war drei Tage nicht sehend." There are only three minute

Example 4.14a. "Wachet auf!"—unrevised

changes to the vocal line. The only other revision is found in the final Simrock version. At the end of the recitative, instead of closing with the customary dominant-tonic cadence, Mendelssohn altered the ending to conclude on the dominant, delaying the tonic chord until the beginning of the ensuing aria. This change creates a stronger and smoother connection between the recitative and aria.

Example 4.14b. "Wachet auf!"—revised

Aria

The revision stages of the aria are far more complex than those of the recitative. That the revisions are more extensive for this aria than for the rest of this first part of scene 2 might be explained by Fanny Hensel's evaluation of this scene, for which Mendelssohn had asked his sister.[13] On 4 February 1836 she wrote: "The first one and the following chorus, chorale and second recitative are grand and beautiful and I wouldn't want to omit any of them. The entire first part of the aria in b minor, from "Herr, thue meine Lippen auf" through the *tempo primo*, is marvelous. I find the return of the words weak. The ending is again very lovely."[14]

Fanny Hensel's main complaint is the transition from the B section to the return of the A section of this da capo aria. A look at the revisions of this aria will show that Mendelssohn took his sister's criticism's seriously. Table 4.17 shows the revision stages of "Gott sei mir gnädig."

Table 4.17. Revision Stages of "Gott sei mir gnädig"

1. MN53I	151-154ac	+	[155-156]	+	157-158ac
2. MN53II	151-154pc	+	[155-156]	+	157-158pc
3. MN55ac					
4. MN55pc					
PS-NYPL					
5. MN53III	151-154pc	+	155-156ac	+	157-158pc
6. MN53IV	151-158pc				
Simrock					

Most of the revisions can be found in MN53. The most drastic revision of this da capo aria is the replacement of the B section. Unfortunately, only six crossed-out measures of the beginning (see Figure 4.9) and three measures of the end of the rejected B version are left in MN53. The leaf (type C paper) containing the rest of the B section was removed and replaced by a different B section, written on type B paper, suggesting that this new B section was composed later than the rest of the movement. Presumably, Mendelssohn agreed with his sister's

Figure 4.9. MN53, p. 154.

remarks about the weakness of the end of the B section. He also realized, however, that the problem of this movement was the whole B section. Even though the rejected B section changed meter (6/8) and tempo
(Allegro moderato), it did not change the lyrical character of the aria
and therefore did not provide the needed contrast. The new B section,
however, turns the aria into a dramatic movement; Mendelssohn indi-

cated "quasi Recit." over the beginning of the B section, which becomes an energetic outburst of Paul as he dedicates his life to mission,
saying, "Denn ich will die Überträter deiner Wege lehren, daß sich die
Sünder zu dir bekehren." Mendelssohn realized the importance of this
line as it displays the first fruits of repentance, the apostle's readiness
and eagerness to serve God by sharing the Gospel. It also makes the
return of the contrasting lyric A section very effective.

It is MN55 that actually contains the earliest version of the newer
B section, while MN53 shows a revised version of MN55. Most of the
corrections are found in the vocal line, and they aim at a more direct
expression of the text's word accents and the flow of the sentence (see
Examples 4.15a and b).

Example 4.15a. MN55, "Gott sey mir gnädig"

Example 4.15b. MN53, "Gott sey mir gnädig"

There are also two structural changes toward the end of the B section.
First Mendelssohn cut two measures of instrumental interlude, making
the final statement of Paul "Herr thue meine Lippen auf" seem more
spontaneous. At the very end of the B section Mendelssohn then repeated "daß mein Mund deinen Ruhm verkündige," highlighting the
impact of Jesus' appearance on Paul's life. Mendelssohn copied the ex-

tra measures at the end of the B section in pencil. The pencil revisions that started with "Wachet auf!" actually continue from here through the remainder of the piece in MN55. These pencil corrections reflect one layer of revision that took place fairly late. Most of these also appear in MN53, where they are actually made in ink.

There are surprisingly few revisions to the A sections of this aria. The corrections mostly are simplifications in the instrumental parts to keep the emphasis clearly on the vocal line.

Paul's Baptism

Overview

The last scene of the first part of the oratorio is a direct continuation of the previous scene. In some ways Mendelssohn treats Paul's baptism as part of his conversion. The previous scene ended with the expression of repentance and his willingness to serve God. It is in this baptism scene, however, that God completes the conversion process through the forgiveness of Paul's sins, expressed in Paul's aria, "Ich danke dir Herr, mein Gott," and the renewing of Paul's mind through the opening of his eyes to the truth, which is Jesus, the Christ (Acts 9:22, used in the last recitative of part 1). Table 4.18 shows the evolution of this scene as it appears in all the textual and musical sources.

Recitatives

MN28 contains a recitative with a different text from all the other musical sources. In this rejected recitative, Paul declares Jesus as the Christ to the unbelieving Jews. The recitative is followed by stanzas 2 and 3 of the chorale "Ein feste Burg." Since the first, unrevised c. 27 draft contains a similar recitative followed by "Ein fest Burg" to close off part 1, it seems safe to assume that the recitative and chorale in MN28 were originally intended to close part 1 of the oratorio. Perhaps Mendelssohn felt that these two movements of MN28 were not convincing textually or musically, because he did not use any aspect from these rejected movements in the later versions.

The first of the two recitatives used eventually in this scene underwent a heavy revision process (see Table 4.19).

Table 4.18. Sources of Part 1, Scene 4

		Libretto sources			
FMB—MDM c.42	Fürst—d. 53, no. 87; d. 30, no. 211	Marx—d. 53, no. 88	FMB—d.30, no. 211; Schubring's comments	FMB—c. 27, p. 28r-30v (ac)	FMB—c. 27, p. 28r-30v (pc)
Der Herr und Ananias (from Acts 9:10-17) Saulus allein (Acts 9:9)	Stimme des Herrn: "Anania!" Ananias: "Hier bin ich, Herr"	Rec.: "Es war aber ein Jünger" Chor 1: "Ich bin das A und das O"	Da sprach der Herr: Ananias etc.	[Rec.:] "Da sprach der Herr zu Ananias" [Rec.:] "Und Ananias ging hin"	[Rec.:] "Es war aber ein Jünger" [Rec.:] "Und Ananias ging hin"
Lange Arie und Rec.—Ananias und Saulus (Acts 9:17)	Ananias: "Lieber Bruder Saul"	Chor 2 dazu: "Amen! Lob und Ehre"		[?] "Herr, Herr verwirf mich nicht"	
Ananias spricht die Worte der Taufe	[Rec.:] "Und alsbald fiel es von seinen Augen"	Rec.: "Und alsbald fiel es von seinen Augen"	[Rec.:] "Und alsbald fiel es von seinen Augen"	[?] "Siehe, ich taufe dich"	[Rec.:] "Und alsbald fiel es von seinen Augen"
Chor der Jnger ermunternd (?)	Ananias: "Gott unserer Väter hat dich"	Paulus: "Jauchzet ihr Himmel"	Paulus: "Jauchzet ihr Himmel"	[?:] "Jauchzet ihr Himmel"	[?:] "Die Nacht ist vergangen"
Paulus predigt	Paulus: "Herr, du hast Worte des ewigen Lebens"		Chor: "Ist das nicht der zu Jerusalem"	Chor: "Wie, ist das nicht der alle verstörte"	Chor: "Ist das nicht, der alle verstörte"
Das Volk entsetzt sich (Acts 9:21)	Ananias: "Ich taufe dich"		Paulus: "Von Jesu zeugen alle Propheten"	[Paulus:] "Wer an Jesum glaubt"	[Rec.:] "Saulus aber ward"
Solo (Acts 9:15-16)	Paulus: "Das ist je gewißlich wahr"		Chor [unspecified]	Chor: "Will er neue Götter"	Chor: "O welch eine Tiefe"
Schluchor—Lobgesang auf die Wege Gottes	Jünger: "Dem der berschwenglich thun kann"			[Paulus:] "Sein Name wird heißen"; Choral: "Ein feste Burg"	

Continued on next page

(Table 4.18—Continued)

	Musical sources					
MN28	MN55ac/MN53ac	MN55pc/MN53pc	PS-NYPLac	PS-NYPLpc	Program of premier	Simrock
	19. Rec.: "Es war aber ein Jünger"	22. Rec.: "Es war aber ein Jünger"	21. Rec.: "Es war aber ein Jüngling"	21. Rec.: "Es war aber ein Jüngling"	22. Rec.: "Es war aber ein Jünger"	19. Rec.: "Es war aber ein Jünger"
	20. Arie und Chor: "Ich danke dir Herr";	23. Arie und Chor: "Ich danke dir Herr";	22. Arie und Chor: "Ich danke dir Herr";	22. Arie und Chor: "Ich danke dir Herr";	23. Arie und Chor: "Ich danke dir Herr";	20. Arie und Chor: "Ich danke dir Herr";
	Chor: "Der Herr wird die Thränen"	Chor: "Der Herr wird die Thränen"	Chor: "Der Herr wird die Thränen"	Chor: "Der Herr wird die Thränen"	Chor: "Der Herr wird die Thränen"	Chor: "Der Herr wird die Thränen"
	21. Rec.: "Und Ananias ging hin"	24. Rec.: "Und Ananias ging hin"	23. Rec.: "Und Ananias ging hin"	23. "eingelegte Arie"—unknown	24. Rec.: "Und Ananias ging hin"	21. Rec.: "Und Ananias ging hin"
	22. Chor: "O welch eine Tiefe"	25. Chor: "O welch eine Tiefe"	24. Chor: "O welch eine Tiefe"	24. Rec.: "Und Ananias ging hin"	25. Chor: "O welch eine Tiefe"	22. Chor: "O welch eine Tiefe"
				25. Chor: "O welch eine Tiefe"		
28. Rec.: "Die unter euch Gott fürchten"						
Choral: "Mit unsrer Macht" [stanza 2 of "Ein feste Burg"]						

Source: Sposato, Jeffrey, Mendelssohn's Theological Evolution: A Study of Textual Choice and Change in the Composer's Sacred Works.

Table 4.19. Revision Stages of "Es war aber ein Jünger (Jüngling)"

1. MN53I
2. MN53II
MN55I
3. MN53III
MN55II
PS-NYPL
4. Simrock

This recitative consists of a recitative section followed by a short arioso. Most of the revisions are found in the recitative, while most of the arioso remains virtually unchanged. The first three stages show revisions to the vocal line as well as to the harmonization of the first section. The longer the recitative section continues, the more revisions there are (see Examples 4.16a and b). The heaviest corrections are in the last line, starting with "daß er meinen Namen sage." Mendelssohn's main concern was the flow of the recitative; all the corrections to that line help to give it stronger forward motion. Since the first part had just reached its climax in the conversion scene, Mendelssohn must have been concerned about a drop-off in intensity. The rewritten recitative of the Simrock version—after the first performance in Düsseldorf—gives evidence for this claim. The last line of text of the first section is cut completely (see Example 4.16c). The recitative section is shortened from 13 to 3 measures; the arioso style is extended to the beginning of the direct speech. As in the previous recitatives containing direct speech, Mendelssohn again used different vocal parts for the narrator and—in this case—the voice of God in a dream.

Mendelssohn changed the instrumentation twice; while the first extant version uses strings, the revised second version uses clarinets, horns, and bassoons. The change to the less common woodwinds could be explained by Mendelssohn's goal to keep the momentum of the scene going; the change of tone color would help in sustaining the listener's interest.

The second recitative consists of three sections: recitative, aria, recitative. Table 4.20 shows the revision process of "Und Ananias ging hin."

Example 4.16a. MN53I, “Es war aber ein Jüngling”

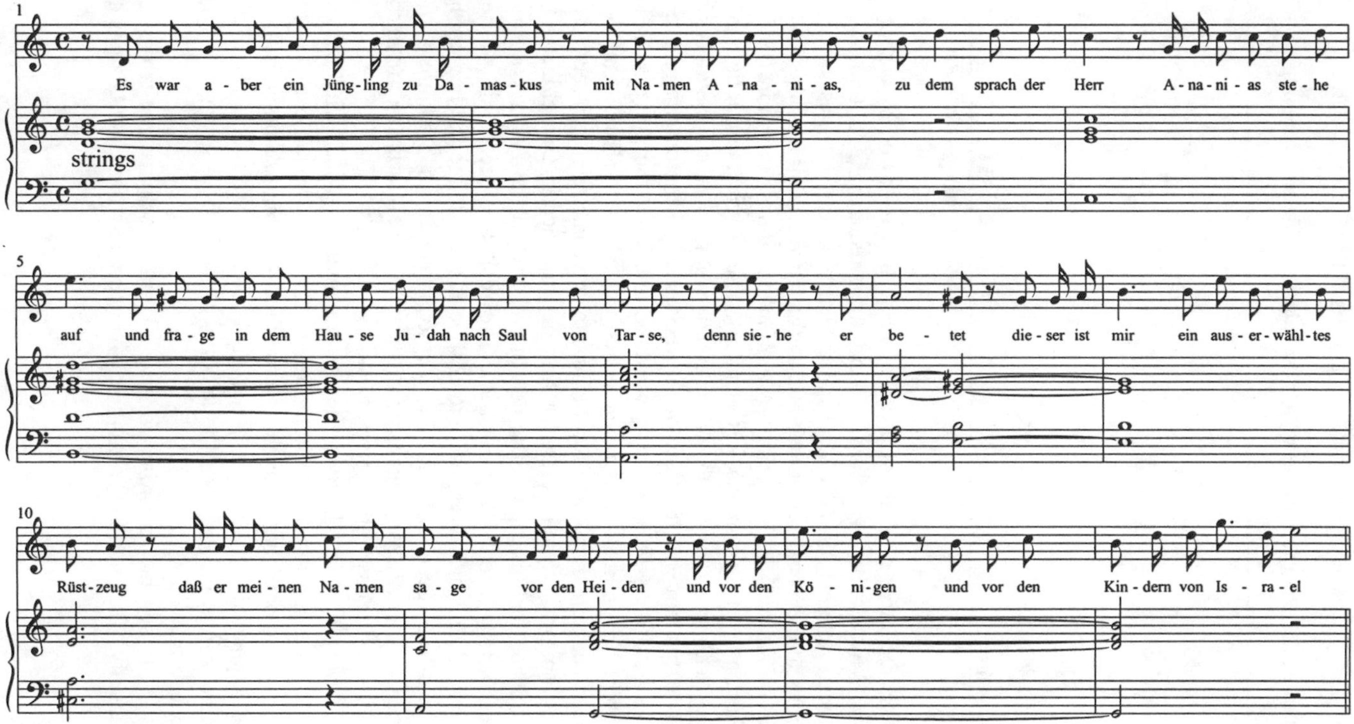

Example 4.16b. MN53III, "Es war aber ein Jüngling"

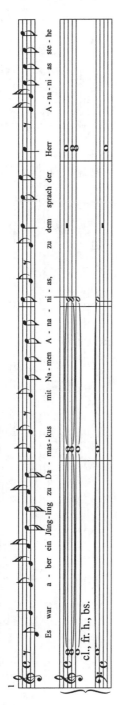

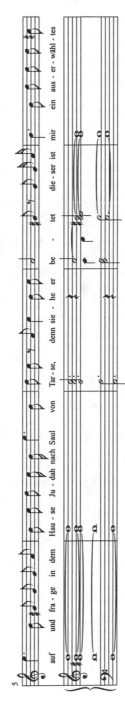
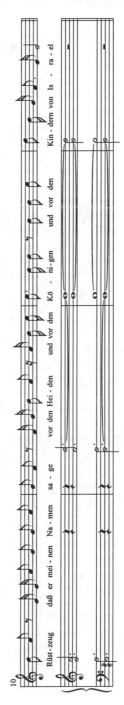

Example 4.16c. Simrock, "Es war aber ein Jüngling"

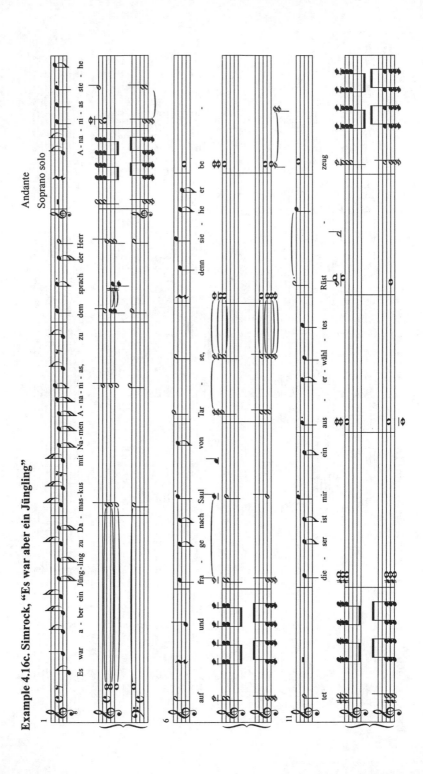

Table 4.20. Revision Stages of "Und Ananias ging hin"

1. MN53I
2. MN53II
3. MN55I
4. MN55II
5. MN53III
6. PS-NYPL
7. Simrock

Although the revision process of the vocal lines of the first two sections was virtually completed after the second stage, the third section underwent drastic changes over the next five stages in its text, structure, and melodic line.

Examples 4.17a-e show five different versions of the last section of this recitative. Two text variants are used; the first part of the text is the same, the endings are different. MN53I/II (stages 1-2, Example 4.17a); MN55I/II (stage 3-4, Example 4.17b); and the published Simrock (stage 7, Example 4.17e) version use a shorter text, which merely states at the end that Paul testified that Jesus was the Christ. In MN53III (stage 5, Example 4.17c) and PS-NYPL (stage 6, Example 4.17d) the words of Paul's testimony are given using Romans 7:25a, 8:2. In both of these instances Mendelssohn assigned the bass to Paul's testimony, while the rest of the recitative is sung by the soprano. While the distribution of dialogue to different vocal parts is consistent with Mendelssohn's usual revisions, the last revision, which cuts Paul's sung testimony, seems at first to be unusual. A closer look at the function of Paul's testimony in this scene, however, explains Mendelssohn's decision to use the shorter text of the earlier revision stages. The words of Paul's testimony do not increase the intensity level of this scene. At this point of the oratorio the exact content of Paul's testimony of Jesus as the Christ is not as important as the fact that he was eager to share it. In fact, by inserting the words of Paul's testimony, Mendelssohn added unimportant details in the dramatic aspects of the story line. This is presumably why Mendelssohn cut Paul's spoken words in the final version.

Another interesting revision is the introduction of the head motif of the final chorus of part 1 of the oratorio, "O welch eine Tiefe" (mm. 4-5 of Example 4.17c, MN53III). By doing so, Mendelssohn emphasized

Example 4.17a. MN53II, "Und Ananias ging hin"

Example 4.17b. MN55II, "Und Ananias ging hin"

Example 4.17c. MN53III, "Und Ananias ging hin"

Example 4.17d. PS-NYPL, "Und Ananias ging hin"

Example 4.17e. Simrock, "Und Ananias ging hin"

the text of the preceding phrase of the recitative, "und ließ sich taufen" ("and was baptized") without changing the vocal line. This revision has to be seen as a direct response to Fanny Hensel's comments on this recitative, "And finally still I want to express my opposition to a passage in the last soprano recitative: the musical treatment of 'und ging hin und liess sich taufen' doesn't measure up to the importance of the text."[15] In both recitatives Mendelssohn made adjustments that affect the intensity level of the scene; his revisions either heighten the intensity or keep it from decreasing. The fact that many times key adjustments were made after the first performance shows the importance of the premiere on the revision process.

Aria with Chorus

The aria with chorus, "Ich danke dir Herr," is heavily revised. Table 4.21 traces the stages of revision.

Table 4.21. Revision Stages of "Ich danke dir Herr"

1. MN53I	161-179I
2. MN53II	161-179II
3. MN55I	
4. MN53III	161-170aIII + 172-179III
MN55II	
PS-NYPL	
5. Simrock	

The revisions from the first to the second stage are numerous, serving the same purpose as seen before in the other movements—to increase clarity and focus. To make the counterpoint more transparent, Mendelssohn omitted voices (see Figure 4.10). The alto and instruments were dropped as the soprano enters with main subject (see Figure 4.11, horns were lightened). Redundant measures, harmonically (see Figures 4.11) as well as melodically (see Figure 4.12), were cut in order to tighten the structure of the movement. Syllables were dropped and adjusted in order to create longer melismas, thus creating a lighter, more transparent texture (see Figure 4.13).

Figure 4.10. MN53, p. 167.

Figure 4.11. MN53, p. 165.

Figure 4.12. MN53, p. 163.

Figure 4.13. MN53, p. 166.

The corrections of stages 2 and 3 focus primarily on one section, the fugato on the second subject of this double fugue. Table 4.22 shows the lengths of the different sections of "Ich danke dir Herr." The Fugato II section was cut twice, shrinking from approximately 30 measures to 24 and then to 15 measures. This change makes the second subject subordinate to the first subject and gives the piece a clearer focus.

Table 4.22. Structural Divisions of "Ich danke dir Herr"

	Aria	Fugato	Fugato II	Fugato III
MN53II	46 mm.	38 mm.	ca. 30 mm.	43 mm.
MN55I	46 mm.	38 mm.	24 mm.	43 mm.
MN53III/ MN55II/ Simrock	46 mm.	38 mm.	15 mm.	43mm.

It is worthwhile to trace the revision process of the fugato II section in MN53 and MN55 in detail. We do not have the complete fugato II section of MN53I/II because of a paste-over; page 172 is a paste-over covering two-thirds of page 170 (see Figure 4.14). The next page (173) and the first two measures of page 174 are crossed out completely. MN55I shows a shortened fugato II section. This shortened version, however, did not just cut a few measures. Mendelssohn rewrote the crossed-out section of MN53I/II in MN55I. Since there is no evidence of another orchestral score, it seems plausible that Mendelssohn might have made these corrections while producing the piano-vocal score MN55. Eventually Mendelssohn decided to shorten and revise the second fugato section once again, which he then did in the orchestral score; all these new corrections were then transferred into MN55 in pencil.

The revision process of the second fugato section of this movement exemplifies the importance of MN55 to the revision process. MN55 is not merely a piano reduction of a particular version in orchestral score format; creating the piano-vocal score became an active part of the revision process.

Figure 4.14. MN53, p. 172.

Chorus

The chorus "O welch eine Tiefe" underwent a difficult revision process. Table 4.23 shows the revision stages.

Table 4.23. Revision Stages of "O welch ein Tiefe"

1. MN53I
2. MN53II
3. MN55I
4. MN55II
MN53III
PS-NYPL
5. Simrock

Almost all of the corrections of this chorus are found in two sources—MN53 and MN55. Two of the three paste-overs in MN53 are found in this movement. Both paste-overs shorten the movement drastically. A comparison of the different stages contained in MN53 and MN55 with the Simrock version of this rondo-form design (ABACDCA) shows that most of the cuts were made in the second half of the movement. The imbalance in the proportions of the earlier versions explains the cuts. In MN53I/II the A ("O welch eine Tiefe") and B ("Wie gar unbegreif-lich") sections of this rondo-form design combine for only 77 measures, while sections C ("Ihm sei Ehre") and D ("Amen") cover 114 measures. Mendelssohn cut 39 measures of MN53I/II to arrive at a very symmetrical structure, with section A and B consisting of 74 measures and sections C and D of 72 measures.

The process of shortening sections C and D by a combined 42 measures, however, was quite complex. Mendelssohn did not cut all the necessary measures in one stage but rather took five layers of revision to do so. The largest cut appears in section C. The stages of the shortening process of this particular section exemplify the types of revisions found in this movement; Examples 4.18a-c display the different layers of revision.

Example 4.18a shows stage 1 (MN53I); Example 4.18b, stage 3 (MN55I); and Example 4.18c, stage 4 (MN53III/55II) of the chorus. The small notes in Example 4.18a are taken from MN55 and represent what appears to be underneath the paste-over. Mendelssohn switched back and forth between MN53 and MN55 in the revision process. In the earlier revisions he only cut a few measures of this section, leading to version MN55I. Mendelssohn eventually decided to shorten this section more drastically. It seems that he worked out the cuts in MN55 using pencil; all the revisions from MN55I to MN55II are written in pencil.

Example 4.18a. MN53I, "O welch eine Tiefe"

Continued on next page

Example 4.18b. MN55I, "O welch ein Tiefe"

Continued on next page

Example 4.18c. MN53III/55II, "O welch eine Tiefe"

Continued on next page

(Example 4.18a—*Continued*)

(Example 4.18b—*Continued*)

(Example 4.18c—*Continued*)

Continued on next page

Continued on next page

Continued on next page

(*Example 4.18a—Continued*)

(*Example 4.18b—Continued*)

(*Example 4.18c—Continued*)

He then transferr̶e̶d the changes into MN53. The cuts were so extensive
that a paste-over was the most convenient solution.

Notes

1. Felix Mendelssohn, *Briefwechsel zwischen Felix Mendelssohn und J.
Schubring zugleich ein Beitrag zur Geschichte des Oratoriums*, ed. Julius
Schubring (Leipzig: Duncker & Humblot, 1892), 6 August 1834 79: Übrigens
bin ich heute sehr melancholisch, wie seit mehreren Tagen, wo ich complett
brach liege, und gar nichts schreibe, ob aus Hitze oder Schwüle oder sonst, das
weiß ich nicht. Nun ist der erste Theil des Paulus beinahe fertig, und ich stehe
davor wie die Kuh und kann nicht in das neue Thor, und mache ihn eben doch
nicht fertig—nämlich die Ouverture fehlt noch, und es ist ein schweres Stück.
Unmittelbar nach den Worten des Herrn bei der Bekehrung habe ich einen
großen Chor: "mache dich auf, werde Licht" u.s.w. Jes. 60, 1-2 eintreten lassen,
den ich bis jetzt für den besten Moment im ersten Theil halte.
2. Julius Schubring, *Briefwechsel zwischen Felix Mendelssohn und J.
Schubring zugleich ein Beitrag zur Geschichte des Oratoriums*, 51-52: Einen
Einleitungschor halte ich für nothwendig. Eine besondere Overtüre weniger.
Die Händelsche Art von Adagio und Fuge ist nur zu abgedroschen, steht auch
meist ohne innere Bedeutung da (nicht in allen). Und ich glaube, ihr Musiker
kommt zu leicht in Versuchung, euch in die Musik an sich zu vertiefen,
worüber dann die kirchliche Bedeutung des Oratoriums verlorengeht. Schwebt
Dir aber etwas vor, was hinpaßt, was etwa z. B. die Zeit der ersten Christenge-
meinde, vor Stephanus Tod, andeuten könnte—ein heiliges Pfingstfest, wo der
Geist ausgegossen wird— nach Ap. Gesch. cap. 2, was wohl viel musikalisches
in sich enthält—oder solche Stellen wie cap. 2, 42-47 oder 4, 32 oder auch ein
Anklang an die vorhergehenden Verfolgungen cap. 4 und 5 zusammen mit der
helfenden Kraft Gottes und mit dem Gebet der Gemeinde c. 4, 24-31—kannst
Du dich mit irgend so etwas recht befreunden, so würde das eine schöne Einlei-
tung sein zu einem Anfangschor der Art, wie ich Dir früher vorgeschlagen
habe. Freilich kann eine Overtüre auch Andeutungen auf das Stück hin enthal-
ten.
3. Felix Mendelssohn, *A Life in Letters*, ed. Rudolf Elvers, trans. by
Craig Tomlinson (New York: Fromm, 1986), 201.
4. See Douglass Seaton, "A Study of a Collection of Mendelssohn's
Sketches and Other Autograph Material," Ph.D. diss., Columbia University,
1977, 4.
5. Julius Schubring, *Briefwechsel zwischen Felix Mendelssohn und J.
Schubring zugleich ein Beitrag zur Geschichte des Oratoriums*, 33.
6. Arntrud Kurzhals-Reuter, *Die Oratorien Felix Mendelssohn Bar-
tholdys:Untersuchungen zur Quellenlage, Entstehung, Gestaltung und Überlieferung*, (Tutzing: Hans Schneider, 1978), 59.
7. Personal correspondence with John Michael Cooper.

8. There is a detailed discussion of this draft in Arntrud Kurzhals-Reuter, *Die Oratorien Felix Mendelssohn Bartholdys: Untersuchungen zur Quellenlage, Entstehung, Gestaltung und Überlieferung*, 97-101.

9. New American Standard Version.

10. Felix Mendelssohn, *Letters from 1833 to 1847*, ed. Paul and Carl Mendelssohn-Bartholdy; trans. by Lady Wallace (London: Longman, Green and Co., 1890), 46.

11. See the discussion above of the use of the chorale tune in the overture, pp. 56-58.

12. For a detailed discussion see Arntrud Kurzhals-Reuter, *Die Oratorien Felix Mendelssohn Bartholdys:Untersuchungen zur Quellenlage, Entstehung, Gestaltung und Überlieferung*, 101-102.

13. Felix Mendelssohn, *Letters from 1833 to 1847*, 30 January 1836, 95.

14. Fanny Hensel, *The Letters of Fanny Hensel to Felix Mendelssohn*, ed. and trans. by Marcia J. Citron (New York: Pendragon Press, 1987), 199.

15. Fanny Hensel, *The Letters of Fanny Hensel to Felix Mendelssohn*, 209.

Chapter 5

Compositional Process in Individual Movements of Part 2

Opening

Overview

The second part of the oratorio starts with a big five-part chorus. A short introduction is followed by a full-fledged double fugue. The reason for such an enormous opening chorus can be found in the tradition of having lengthy intermissions between parts of oratorios.[1] Mendelssohn used this large-scale chorus to help the audience focus on the story once again. He had difficulty, however, in finding the right beginning for the second part of the oratorio, because MN55 contains three different openings on two different texts.

Text

Table 5.1 shows the opening texts found in all sources. Of the version in MN55 on the first text, "Die Nacht ist vergangen," only one page is left (see Figure 5.1). it is found on the verso side of the last page of music of part 1. Since Mendelssohn could not remove it easily, he crossed out the whole page. Surprisingly, this rejected movement was reused years later as chorus no. 7 in Mendelssohn's *Lobgesang*. The text suggestion for this rejected movement only appears in the second of the c. 27 drafts; in the first of these librettos Mendelssohn used yet another text, "Nun sind die Reiche der Welt." Mendelssohn never numbered this rejected movement, which suggests that the numbering of movements was not done until after the movements were written.

Table 5.1. Sources of the Opening Chorus of Part 2

Libretto sources							
FMB—c. 27, p. 28r-30v			FMB—c. 27, p. 31r-32r				
[Chor:] "Nun sind die Reiche der Welt"			Chor: "Die Nacht ist vergangen"				
Musical sources							
MN55ac	MN55pc	PS-NYPLac	PS-NYPLpc	MN54	Program of premier	Simrock
Chor: "Die Nacht ist vergangen"	26. Chor: "Der Erdkreis ist nun des Herrn"	25. Chor: "Der Erdkreis ist nun des Herrn"	26. Chor: "Der Erdkreis ist nun des Herrn"	26. Chor: "Der Erdkreis ist nun des Herrn"	26. Chor: "Der Erdkreis ist nun des Herrn"	24. Chor: "Der Erdkreis ist nun des Herrn"

Source. Sposato, Jeffrey, *Mendelssohn's Theological Evolution: A Study of Textual Choice and Change in the Composer's Sacred Works*, Ph.D. diss., Brandeis University, 1999.

The decision to change the opening text from Romans 13:12, a general verse about the sanctification process of a Christian, to Revelation 11:15 and 15:4, verses about the supremacy of Christ over all the earth, seems persuasive, because the rejected text is reflective of the first part of the oratorio, while the second choice anticipates Paul's missionary work. The content of the verses from Revelation is similar to that of his earlier choice, "Nun sind die Reiche," from Acts 11:15, 17.

Introduction

Even after Mendelssohn replaced the opening movement with a new one on a different text, he was not satisfied with the opening. He revised the introduction of the opening chorus by inserting a page at the beginning of the movement (see Figure 5.2). The replaced introduction on the following page is crossed out (see Figure 5.3). Mendelssohn decided to have a longer, bigger introduction. While the beginning of the inserted, revised introduction is almost identical with the previous one, the second part of the introduction is quite different. It is prolonged

Figure 5.1. MN55, p. 51v.

through short imitative entrances and through a restatement of the first part of the introduction. Mendelssohn later crossed out two repetitious measures to tighten the structure of the longer introduction. The last revision of the introduction is found in the Simrock version (see Exam-

Figure 5.2. MN55, p. 52v.

ple 5.1). Mendelssohn changed the orchestral accompaniment in measures 6 and 10 to match the opening motive of the choir, unifying the introduction musically.

Figure 5.3. MN55, p. 53r.

Double Fugue

All the revisions made to the double fugue are found in MN55. PS-NYPL is a clean copy of MN55, and MN54 contains few minor revisions. MN55 contains numerous textual as well as contrapuntal revisions—all are minor, however; they are the same types of revisions

Example 5.1. Simrock, "Der Erdkreis ist nun des Herrn"

found in earlier contrapuntal movements of part 1. The textual revisions are all syllable adjustments either to fit the text better with the music or to synchronize the text of the different vocal parts. The musical revisions are all designed to make the contrapuntal texture more transparent. Example 5.2 shows the tenor line being crossed out as the second sopranos enter with important thematic material.

Example 5.2. MN55 "Der Erdkreis ist nun des Herrn"

Paul and Barnabas Are Sent

Overview

This scene marks the starting point of Paul's ministry as he is called by God and sent out by the Church to be a missionary. Table 5.2 shows the text and music sources for this first scene of part 2 of the oratorio.

Recitatives

The first of the two recitatives does not show many revisions. As was the case with the opening chorus, most of the revisions take place in MN55. MN55 contains the earliest extant version of "Und Paulus kam zu der Gemeinde." Table 5.3 shows the revision stages of this first recitative.

Altogether there are only six minor revisions made, and MN55 contains five of them. The changes in the vocal part make the recitative more expressive (compare mm. 3, 6, and 8 in Examples 5.3a and b). The other two revisions in MN55 are found in the accompaniment; one prolongs a chord, the other redistributes a chord and adds a passing tone.

Table 5.2. Sources of Part 2, Scene 1

Libretto sources	
FMB—c. 27, p. 28r-30v	FMB—c. 27, p. 31r-32r
[Rec.:] "Und Paulus kam zu der Gemeinde" Arie mit Chor: "Wie lieblich sind die Füße"	[Rec.:] "Und Paulus kam zu der Gemeinde" "So sind wir nun Botschafter" Arie mit Chor: "Wie lieblich sind die Füße"—Crossed out

Musical sources				
MN55ac/ MN54ac	MN55pc/ MN54pc	PS-NYPL	Program of premier	Simrock
27. Rec.: "Und Paulus kam zu der Gemeinde"	27. Rec.: "Und Paulus kam zu der Gemeinde"	27. Rec.: "Und Paulus kam zu der Gemeinde"	27. Rec.: "Und Paulus kam zu der Gemeinde"	27. Rec.: "Und Paulus kam zu der Gemeinde"
28. Duettino: "So sind wir nun Botschafter"	28. Duettino: "So sind wir nun Botschafter"	28. Duettino: "So sind wir nun Botschafter"	28. Duettino: "So sind wir nun Botschafter"	28. Duettino: "So sind wir nun Botschafter"
29. Chor: "Wie lieblich sind die Boten"	29. Chor: "Wie lieblich sind die Boten"	29. Chor: "Wie lieblich sind die Boten"	29. Chor: "Wie lieblich sind die Boten"	26 Chor: "Wie lieblich sind die Boten"
30[a.] Rec.: "Und wie sie ausgesandt"	30[a.] Rec.: Und wie sie ausgesandt"; Arioso: "Laßt uns singen von der Gnade"	30[a.] Rec.: "Und wie sie ausgesandt"	30[a.] Rec.: "Und wie sie ausgesandt"; Arioso: "Laßt uns singen von der Gnade"	27 Rec.: "Und wie sie ausgesandt"; Arioso: "Laßt uns singen von der Gnade"

Source. Sposato, Jeffrey, *Mendelssohn's Theological Evolution: A Study of Textual Choice and Change in the Composer's Sacred Works.*

Table 5.3. Revision Stages of "Und Paulus kam zu der Gemeinde"

1. MN55ac

2. MN55pc

   MN53

   PS-NYPL

3. Simrock

The last change was made in the Simrock version; Mendelssohn revoiced another chord to approach the top note of the following chord from the leading tone.

The revision process of the second recitative, "Und wie sie ausgesandt," is more complicated than that of the first one. As Mendelssohn

Example 5.3a. MN55ac, "Und Paulus kam zu der Gemeinde"

Example 5.3b. MN55pc, "Und Paulus kam zu der Gemeinde"

had done once before with a recitative in part 1, he split "Und wie sie ausgesandt" into two short recitatives, inserting the arioso "Laßt uns singen von der Gnade." Mendelssohn must have added the arioso quite late in the revision process, because MN54 and MN55 both bear witness to this revision, and because PS-NYPL, usually a clean copy of the revised MN55 version, shows the unrevised single recitative and no arioso. MN55 shows the revision process the most clearly. The page containing the arioso (page 62) was inserted before the complete recitative (see Table 5.4). At the top of the page Mendelssohn wrote, "nach nr. 30 'mit Freudigkeit,'" indicating that this arioso is to be sung halfway through the recitative (see Figure 5.4). The page containing the recitative also bears the last three measures of the preceding chorus, "Wie lieblich sind die Boten," which makes the insertion of the arioso even more obvious (see Figure 5.5). Since the verso side of the page containing the recitative already has the next chorus on it ("So spricht

Table 5.4. Foliation of Nos. 29-31 (beg.) in MN55

Page number	Comments	Paper type
58	No. 27 Recit. "Und Paulus kam"	C
	No. 28 Duettino "So sind wir nun Botschafter"	
		C
59	No. 29 Chor "Wie lieblich sind die Boten"	C
		C
60		C
		C
61	paste-over	C
		C
62	No. 30 Arioso "Lasst uns singen von der Gnade"	C
	FMB: "auf no. 30 'mit Freudigkeit'"	
		C
63	No. 30 Recit. "Und wie sie ausgesandt"	B
	~~No. 31~~ Chor "So spricht der Herr"	B
64	No. 31 Recit. "Und sie stellten Paulus nach"	B
		B

der Herr"), Mendelssohn was forced to insert the page containing the arioso before the recitative. The only revisions found in the recitative "Und wie sie ausgesandt" are the necessary adjustments made in the last measure to end the recitative there (see Figure 5.5).

Mendelssohn also inserted the arioso at a later time in MN54. In that manuscript, too, it appears before the recitatives. In MN54, however, the recitatives already appear as two separate recitatives. Between the two recitatives Mendelssohn wrote, "folgt eine Arie" (see Figure 5.6). As was the case in the piano-vocal score, in MN54 Mendelssohn was forced to insert the arioso before the final two measures of the preceding chorus. No further revisions to these recitatives appear in MN54. The Simrock version revises the last measure of the recitative again; there the recitative elides with the arioso.

Arioso

The arioso "Laßt uns singen von der Gnade des Herrn" was probably not inserted into the manuscript until Mendelssohn arrived in Düsseldorf for the rehearsals of the first performance. He wrote to Woringen on 21 April 1836,

Figure 5.4. MN 55, p. 62r.

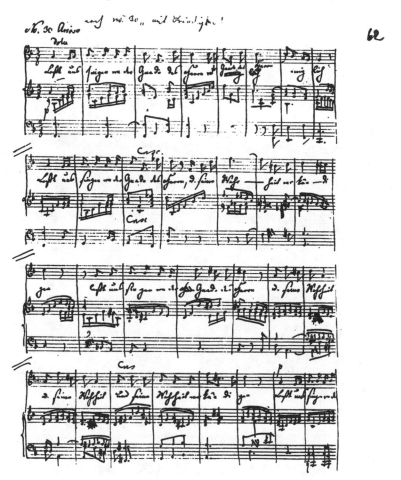

With this I send you the rest of part two of the full score. Have it
brought to the copyist right away, and tell him that the second aria,
which is to follow the recitative no. 32, has to be inserted; as is the
case with another aria, which is to follow no. 30. I will bring both
arias myself, and then they can be written out and placed into the

Figure 5.5. MN55, p. 63r.

parts. The copyist must do his work carefully, since the full score is not written well; it would be best, as I wrote earlier, if Schauseil could copy the parts, if he is still in Düsseldorf.[2]

While the arioso—together with the other previously mentioned aria— might be the last movement to have found its place into the oratorio, it

Figure 5.6. MN54, p. 35

might not have been the last one composed. Both manuscript versions of "Laß uns singen von der Gnade" were written on paper of type C. Mendelssohn used type C paper in the earlier versions but not for his later revisions. He may have run out of time and used an aria that he composed earlier.

Not many revisions are found in MN55 and MN54. A few minute adjustments are made to the vocal line as well as to the text distribution. In the orchestral score in MN54, Mendelssohn made the sound more transparent by taking out some doublings of instruments.

Mendelssohn was not satisfied with the arioso, however, as the revisions in the Simrock version show. Mendelssohn made structural changes and revised the vocal as well as the instrumental parts. In the B section of this short arioso in ABA form, Mendelssohn added four measures in the Simrock version (compare the B section as shown in Examples 5.4a and b). By adding four measures to the first part of the

Example 5.4a. MN55, "Laßt uns singen von der Gnade des Herrn"

Example 5.4b. Simrock, "Laßt und singen von der Gnade des Herrn"

B section, Mendelssohn achieved a better balance in relation to the second part. In the second half of the B section he then changed the text to

leave only one text repetition—as is the case in the first part—rather than two repetitions. Mendelssohn made exactly the same type of revision in the returning A section, also adding four measures.

The addition of eight measures is very substantial for such a short arioso. In fact, the expansion of "Laßt uns singen von der Gnade" changes the function of the arioso in this scene. In MN55, the earliest version, the arioso is merely a more expressive moment within a longer recitative; everything is sung by the soprano soloist. In MN54 Mendelssohn actually divided the recitative into two by having the tenor soloist sing what had been a continuation of the recitative in MN55. In the published version one would never know that these two recitatives originally belonged together, since the second recitative received a new number. Mendelssohn purposely assigned a new number to the second recitative to give a clearer sense of scene structure: in the earlier versions the recitative elided scenes 1 and 2, whereas in the Simrock version a clear break is established between the two scenes.

Duettino

The duettino has only two minor revisions; both of these are deletions of doublings within the orchestral accompaniment in MN54, improving the transparency of the orchestral sound.

Chorus

The revision stages of "Wie lieblich sind die Boten" are not difficult to ascertain. Table 5.5 shows the layers of revisions. As can be seen in Table 5.5, most of the revisions are found in MN55. As Table 5.4 shows, "Wie lieblich sind die Boten" contains a paste-over page (61r); also, the arioso "Laßt uns singen von der Gnade" was inserted between 61v and 63r as 62r-62v. The continuous page numbering, which is in Mendelssohn's hand, shows that he numbered MN55 very late in the revision process.

The paste-over demonstrates Mendelssohn's striving for a more precise and tighter movement structure. The adjacent measures of the previous and following pages are crossed out, and the measures on the paste-over page are spaced out more, which means that the paste-over page contains a shorter passage than the unrevised version that included the crossed-out measures on the adjacent pages. Mendelssohn made two more cuts, four and one measures, respectively, in other places. The four-measure cut shown in Example 5.5 displays how and why these cuts were made. There are two main reasons for the cut: (1) The first section of this ABA form was disproportionately long compared to the other two and needed to be shortened to create a more balanced movement; and (2) earlier in this section Mendelssohn had already used the complete theme imitatively, making a third complete imitative statement of the theme seem redundant in this context.

Other revisions are mostly syllable adjustments. As in previous movements, adjustments were made to create longer melismas for more transparency or to synchronize the text of different vocal parts to improve the clarity of the words (see Figure 5.7).

Table 5.5. Revision Stages of "Wie lieblich sind die Boten"

1. MN55I	59r-60v,ac	+	x	+	61v,ac-y		
2. MN55II	59r-60v,pc	+	61r	+	61v,pc-y		
3. MN55III	59r-61v,pc					+	63r
4. MN54ac							
5. MN54pc							
PS-NYPL							
6. Simrock							

Paul Is Rejected by the Jews

Overview

As discussed previously, the second scene was not clearly separated from the first scene until after the first performance, when Mendelssohn revised the oratorio for the last time. All of the earlier versions elided scenes 1 and 2 through a long recitative, which Mendelssohn ultimately divided into two separate recitatives. As Table 5.6 shows, the numbering reflects the elision of the scenes; all the versions before the Simrock edition continue the previous number through what finally became the beginning of the second scene.

Mendelssohn pieced together the text for this scene from different libretto sources: the chorus "Ist das nicht" first appeared in Fürst's

draft, the use of a chorale was suggested by Schubring in response to
Mendelssohn's draft sent to him. It is again in the c.27 drafts that Men-
delssohn settled on the basic outline for the scene. The text for the aria
"Jerusalem," used in later drafts in the first part of the oratorio during
Stephanus's stoning scene, was originally suggested for this scene by
Marx.

Example 5.5. MN55, "Wie lieblich sind die Boten"

Figure 5.7. MN55, p. 59r.

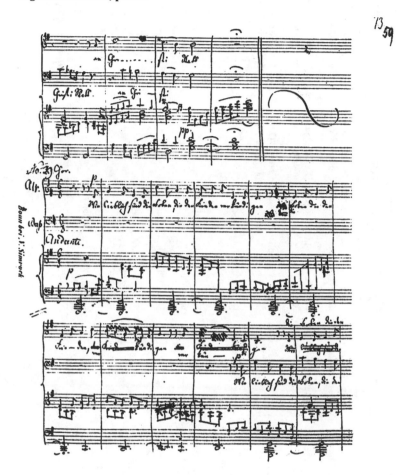

Recitatives

Scene 2 has three short recitatives. The first recitative, "Da aber die Juden das Volk sahen," appeared in the piano-vocal scores of MN55 and PS-NYPL. It actually served as the second part of the last recitative of the previous scene (as discussed above). Mendelssohn made only a few minor revisions to the vocal part (see Figure 5.5).

Table 5.6 Sources of Part 2, Scene 2

		Libretto sources			
FMB—MDM c.42	Fürst—d. 53, no. 87; d. 30, no. 211	Marx—d. 53, no. 88	FMB—d.30, no. 211; Schubring's comments	FMB—c. 27, p. 28r-30v	FMB—c. 27, p. 31r-32r
Acts 9:23-29; 13:2, 45 ["... hielten die Juden einen Rat"]	Paulus: "Wer das Glaubet, da sey der Christ"	Paulus: "Herr, du hast Worte des ewigen Lebens"	Paulus: "Herr, du hast Worte des ewigen Lebens"	[Rec.:] "Da aber die Juden das Volk sahen"	[Rec.:] "Da aber die Juden das Volk sahen"
Trauer um die Ungläubigkeit der Juden (Romans 9:2-3; 10:1-4)	Volk: "Ist das nicht, der zu Jerusalem verstörte"	Judenchor: "Wer sind sie, die einen Gott machen?"	Rec.: "Und sie hielten einen Rath"	[Rec.:] "Paulus aber und Barnabas"	[Rec.:] "Paulus aber und Barnabas"
Er wendet sich den Heiden zu (Acts 13:46-48)	[Rec.:] "Und nach vielen Tagen hielten die Juden"	Rec.: "Und sie hielten einen Rath"	Chor: "Was sollte Gott nach jenem fragen"	Choral: "O treuer Heiland Jesu Christ"	"Ich habe dich den Heiden zum Licht gesetzt"
Und predigt ihnen (Eph. 2:8, 19; 1:3; Phil. 2:15-18)	[Rec.:] "An einem Sabbath kam zusammen"		[Rec.:] "Die Jünger aber retteten ihn"		[Rec.:] "Da es aber die Heiden hörten"
Die Juden verstoßen ihn (Acts 13:50-51)	Paulus und Barnabas: "Euch mußte zuerst das Wort Gottes"		FMB: "Hier ein Choral oder eine Arie"		Choral: "O treuer Heiland Jesu Christ"—crossed out
	Paulus: "Ich sage die Wahrheit"		[Rec.:] "Da aber die Juden"		
	Aria: "Jerusalem"	Paulus: "Jerusalem"	Chor: "So spricht der Herr"		
			[Rec.:] "Paulus aber und Barnabas"		
			Paulus: "Jerusalem"		
			Choral: "O treuer Heiland Jesu Christ"		

Continued on next page

(Table 5.6—Continued)

				Musical sources			
MN19	MN28	MN55ac	MN55pc	PS-NYPL	MN54	Program of premier	Simrock
last page of Bass aria, "Ich habe dich den Heiden"	Rec.: "Die unter euch Gott fürchten"; [Choral: "Ein fest Burg"]		30. cont. Rec.: "Da aber die Juden das Volk sahen"; 31. [crossed out] Chor: "So spricht der Herr"	30. cont. Chor: "So spricht der Herr"	30. cont. Rec.: "Da aber die Juden das Volk sahen"; Chor: "So spricht der Herr"	30. cont. Rec.: "Da aber die Juden das Volk sahen"; Chor: "So spricht der Herr"	28. Rec.: "Da aber die Juden das Volk sahen"/ Coro: "So spricht der Herr"/ Rec.: "Und sie stellten Paulus nach"
		Rec.: "Und sie stellten Paulus nach"; Chor: "Ist das nicht"; [Choral:] "O Jesu Christe"	31. Rec.: "Und sie stellten Paulus nach"; Chor: "Ist das nicht"; [Choral:] "O Jesu Christe"	31. Rec.: "Und sie stellten Paulus nach"; Chor: "Ist das nicht"; Choral: "O Jesu Christe"	31. Rec.: "Und sie stellten Paulus nach"; Chor: "Ist das nicht"; [Choral:] "O Jesu Christe"	31. Rec.: "Und sie stellten Paulus nach"; Chor: "Ist das nicht"; Choral: "O Jesu Christe"	29. Coro: "Ist das nicht"; [Choral:] "O Jesu Christe"
		33. Rec.: "Paulus aber und Barnabas"; FMB: "hier folgt eine Arie"	32. Rec.: "Paulus aber und Barnabas"; FMB: "hier folgt eine Arie"	32. Rec.: "Paulus aber und Barnabas"	32. Rec.: "Paulus aber und Barnabas"; FMB: "hier folgt eine Arie"	32. Rec.: "Da sprach Paulus zu ihnen"; Arie: "Ich habe dich den Heiden"	30. Rec.: "Paulus aber und Barnabas"
							31. Duetto: "Denn also hat uns der Herr geboten"

Source. Sposato, Jeffrey, Mendelssohn's Theological Evolution: A Study of Textual Choice and Change in the Composer's Sacred Works.

The second recitative, "Und sie stellten Paulus nach," is the shortest of this scene. The only revisions are found in MN55 (see Examples
5.6a and b). In measure 4 Mendelssohn moved the vocal part up an octave, creating a more convincing phrase shape.

Example 5.6a. MN55ac, "Und sie stellten Paulus nach"

Example 5.6b. MN55pc, "Und sie stellten Paulus nach"

The third recitative has two different beginnings, textually as well
as musically. MN54 and the program of the premiere start the recitative's text and music differently from the other sources. A first look
seems to indicate that MN54 holds the earlier version, while MN55
contains the revised version, since its beginning is identical with that of
the published version. A closer look, however, shows that the MN55
version was actually written before MN54; a comparison of the ensuing
movements, written on the same bifolio, clearly identifies MN55 as the
earlier version. A change in paper type in both manuscripts indicates
that Mendelssohn either inserted into MN55 and MN54 the pages containing everything from this third recitative to the chorus "Die Götter
sind den Menschen" of the third scene or replaced earlier versions. Table 5.7 shows the stages of revision of this third recitative.

Table 5.7. Revision Stages of "Paul aber und Barnabas/Da sprach Paulus zu ihnen"

1. MN55ac
2. MN55pc
PS-NYPL
3. MN54ac
4. MN54pc
5. Simrock

In the Simrock edition Mendelssohn combined ideas from the earlier versions found in MN55 and MN54 (see Examples 5.7a-c). The most obvious revision is the text change at the beginning of the recitative. Here Mendelssohn went back to his earlier text choice used in MN55, "Paulus aber und Barnabas sprachen frei und öffentlich" ("Paul and Barnabas, however, spoke freely and publicly"). This text talks generically about Paul's and Barnabas's missionary ministry, while the version of the premiere, found in MN54, places Paul—and only Paul—in a specific context: "Da sprach Paul zu ihnen" ("Then Paul spoke to them"). The recitative continues with Paul announcing his intention to preach to the Gentiles, since the Jews were rejecting his message. Mendelssohn probably felt that the more generic version was better suited for this scene, since it implies a prolonged ministry to the Jews rather than only one attempt to reach them. The most obvious musical revision incorporated into the final version is the insertion in MN54 of an instrumental measure (m. 6 of Example 5.7b). This inserted measure brings back the motivic material of the third measure of the recitative. This motivic material appropriately makes reference to the chorus heard earlier, "So spricht der Herr," in which the Jews mock Paul's message.

Choruses

This scene has two choruses. Both of them are turba choruses representing the Jews. In the first, the above-mentioned chorus "So spricht der Herr," all the revisions are found in MN55. As Figure 5.8 shows, Mendelssohn shifted the barlines by two beats, changing the emphasized word from "so" to "Herr," a more effective declamation in this

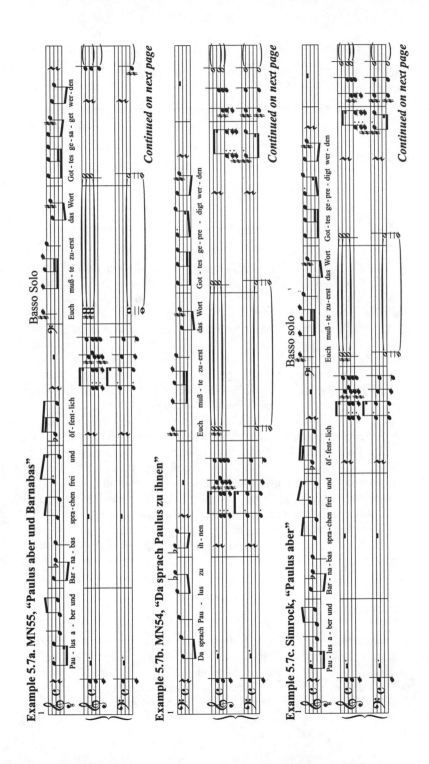

Example 5.7a. MN55, "Paulus aber und Barnabas"

Example 5.7b. MN54, "Da sprach Paulus zu ihnen"

Example 5.7c. Simrock, "Paulus aber"

Continued on next page

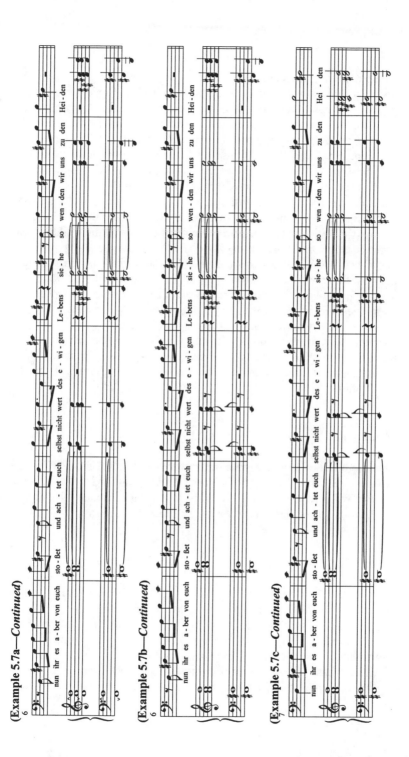

(Example 5.7a—*Continued*)

(Example 5.7b—*Continued*)

(Example 5.7c—*Continued*)

context. Mendelssohn probably made this adjustment just as he was about to begin to write the second system of music. Since this is an important conceptual revision for this movement, one that has a clear impact on the rest of the movement, Mendelssohn was probably in the process of composing it when he made this revision. The other major revisions are found at the bottom of the same page (Figure 5.8). Here Mendelssohn reworked the tenor and bass parts to use the main motivic material once again in the bass part to unify the movement and give it focus. There are no other revisions in the other sources. MN19 contains a sketch of the opening of "So spricht der Herr" (see Example 5.8). Although the initial statement of the theme is the same, the imitative entrances seem unpolished, producing difficult vocal lines.

Even though the second chorus, "Ist das nicht," is much longer than the first one, it also shows traces of revisions only in MN55. There are only two changes. One is a cut of eight measures toward the end of the movement, making the ending more concise and focused. The other revision is a rhythmic change at the words "Weg, weg mit ihm" (see Example 5.9). Mendelssohn pulled the words of the phrase together by taking out the rests between the words "Weg, weg" and "mit ihm." The result is a more focused phrase, with only one strong emphasis on the word "ihm."

Chorale

The chorale shows only three minute voice-leading revisions in MN54 in the vocal parts. The only other revision is found in PS-NYPL; here the top voice (alto) ends on the fifth of the chord rather than on the third, which gives the chorale a stronger sense of finality.

Duet

The duet appears only in the Simrock version. Mendelssohn was not able to finish this movement in time to include it among the manuscripts when he sent them to the copyist.[3] Even in the printed program of the premiere only part of the text of the duet is printed, and the movement is labeled "Arie." Page 10 of MN19 shows the last page of an aria for bass and strings with the text of the duet. Apparently Mendelssohn had previously written an aria with that text but discarded it to

Figure 5.8. MN55, p. 63v.

revise it for the first performance. It is not clear what, if any, movement was performed at the premiere at that spot. The bass aria contained in MN19 has no musical similarities to the duet of the published version.

Example 5.8. MN19, "So spricht der Herr"

Example 5.9a. MN55ac, "Ist das nicht"

Example 5.9b. MN55pc, "Ist das nicht"

Paul's Missionary Work to the Gentiles

Overview

The third scene is the longest and most complex scene of the second part. It consists of two sections: (1) Paul evangelizes the Gentiles, and (2) the Gentiles reject Paul's message. Table 5.8 shows the drafts found in all of the source materials. In the earlier drafts this scene was longer than in the later versions, as they also contained Paul's imprisonment and God's miraculous freeing of Paul and Silas. By combining different parts of different events on Paul's missionary journey, Mendelssohn tried to create one long, continuous scene that would contain all of the important aspects of Paul's ministry: (1) The power of God given to Paul's ministry, exemplified in the healing of a lame man (Acts 14:6-10); (2) the portrayal of the Gentiles' heathen beliefs and their incompatibility with the Gospel, displayed in Paul's and Barnabas's deification (Acts 14:11-13); (3) the preaching of the Gospel by Paul (Acts 14:15 and various Old and New Testament passages); (4) the rejection of the Gospel and Paul's persecution (various passages from Acts); and (5) the ministry of Paul sustained by God, shown in God's miraculous freeing of the incarcerated Paul and Silas and the conversion of the jailer (Acts 16:25-31). Perhaps Mendelssohn realized that this scene was becoming too long, incoherent, and unfocused. At the beginning of the scene Paul was with Barnabas, while at the end of the scene it was Paul and Silas who were freed. Consequently, Mendelssohn removed the prison scene, realizing that God's power in Paul's ministry was shown through the healing of the lame. He also abbreviated the deification of Paul and Barnabas, taking out some of the *Heidenchöre*. MN28 contains much of the rejected material of this scene. The fact that 59 of the 92 pages of rejected material of *Paulus* found in MN28 were part of this scene shows how radical the revision process was that was applied to this scene.

Paul Evangelizes the Gentiles

Introduction

The first part of the scene is one of the most heavily revised sections in the entire oratorio. Changes were made to its overall structure by cutting or replacing movements, both before and after the first performance. Individual movements were also revised substantially.

Table 5.8. Sources of Part 2, Scene 3

		Libretto sources			
FMB—MDM c.42	Fürst—d. 53, no. 87; d. 30, no. 211	Marx—d. 53, no. 88	FMB—d.30, no. 211; Schubring's comments	FMB—c. 27, p. 28r-30v	FMB—c. 27, p. 31r-32r
Er thut ein Wunder (Acts 14:8-11)	[Rec.:] "Und es war ein Mann zu Lystra"	Rec.: "Etliche aber der Epikurer"	[Rec.:] "Und es war ein Mann zu Lystra"	[Rec.:] "Und es war ein Mann zu Lystra"	[Rec.:] "Und es war ein Mann zu Lystra"
Chor und Hymnus (Acts 14:11-13)	Paulus: "Stehe aufrichtig"	Paulus: "Ihr Männer von Athene"	[Chor:] "Kommet herzu"	[Chor:] "Kommet herzu"	[Chor:] "Die Götter sind den Menschen"
Paulus unterbricht sie (Acts 14:15-17)	[Rec.:] "Und er sprang auf"	Rec.: "Da sie solches hören"	[Rec.:] "Und sie nannten Barnabas"	[Chor:] "Denn die Götter sind den Menschen"	[Chor:] "Danket den Göttern"
[Paul's sermon] (Acts 17:22-32)	Griechen: "Die Götter sind den Menschen"	Arie: "Wehe, wehe, die große Stadt"	[Chor:] "Wahrlich dieser ist Zeus"	[Rec.:] "Und die Priester brachten"	[Rec.:] "Und nannten Barnabas Jupiter"
Das Volk: "Was will das werden?"	Ein Grieche: "Wahrlich, dieser ist Zeus"	Rec.: "Da sich aber. . . Und es war ein Mann zu Lystra"	[Rec.:] "Da zerissen die Apostel ihre Kleider"	[Chor:] "Er hält den Himmel"	[Chor:] "Sey uns gnädig, hoher Herrscher"
Paulus heftiger (Jer. 10:3-5)	Ein Anderer: "Wie durch Phrygien einst"	Chor: "Lobsinget mit Psalter"	Arie: "(Denn) der Heiden Götter"	Chor: "Sey uns gnädig Herr"	[Chor:] "Lobt ihn mit Saiten"
Einige wiegeln das Volk auf (Acts 19:26-27)	Paulus und Barnabas: "Ihr Männer, was macht ihr da?"	Rec.: "Und tanzten um sie"	[Rec.:] "Es erhub sich aber"	[Rec.:] "Da zerissen die Apostel"	Mdchenchor: "Danket dem Herrn, dem freundlichen Gott"
Das Volk ["Und als sie das hrten"]	Hymnus: "Heil dir zumeist"	Festhymnus: "Wahrlich dieser ist Zeus"	Chor: "Groß ist die Diana"	[Chor:] "Der Heiden Götter"	[Rec.:] "Ihr Männer was macht ihr da?"
Paulus (Jer. 51:17-18) ["Alle Menschen sind Narren"]	Paulus: "Wir sind auch sterbliche"	Rec.: "Da zerissen die Apostel"	[Rec.:] "Und die ganze Stadt"	[Rec.:] "Es erhub sich aber"	[Chor:] "Der Heiden Götter"
Volk "Groß ist die Diana"	Hymnus: "Grüß auch dir"	Beide: "Ihr Männer"	Duett: "Gelobet sei Gott"	[Chor:] "Groß ist die Diana"	[Rec.:] "Und da sie das sagten"
[Rec.:] Acts 16:22-24 ["Und das Volk ward erregt"]	Paulus und Barnabas: "Ihr Männer, was macht ihr da"	Rec.: "Es erhob sich aber"	Chor: "O wie ist die Barmherzigkeit"	[Rec.:] "Und die ganze Stadt"	[Chor:] "Danket dem Zeus"

Continued on next page

(Table 5.8—*Continued*)

FMB—MDM c.42	Fürst—d. 53, no. 87; d. 30, no. 211	Marx—d. 53, no. 88	FMB—c. 27, p. 28r-30v	FMB—c. 27, p. 31r-32r
Paulus und Silas loben Gott, Duett (2. Co. 4:8-10; Rom. 8:35) Acts 19:11-12 ["Und Gott wirkte nicht geringe Taten"]	Paulus: "Hier bin herdurch gegangen"	Chor: "Groß ist die Diana"	[Chor:] "Groß ist die Diana"	[Rec.:] "Paulus aber sprach: Alle Menschen sind Narren"
	Griechen: "Was will dieser Lotterbube sagen"	Rec.: "Und die ganze Stadt"	[Rec.:] "Und da sie das sagten"	Chor: "Wisset ihr nicht"
	Andere: "Er siehet als wolle er"	Chor: "Groß ist die Diana"	Duett: "Gelobet sei Gott"	[Rec.:] "Und das Volk ward erreget"
	Paulus: "Der Heiden Götter"	Rec.: "Und steinigten Paulus"	[Chor:] "Herr Gott Zebaoth"	[Chor:] "Hier ist des Herren Tempel"
	Aria: "Sie haben Mäuler"	Paulus: "Ach wehe der sündigen Menschen"	[Rec.:] "Schnell aber ward ein großes Erdbeben"	[Rec.:] "Und die Hauptleute"
	Goldschmied: "Ihr sehet und höret"	Rec.: "Und hub an"	[Paulus:] "Thue dir nichts"	Duett: "Gelobet sei Gott"
	Chor der Goldschmiede: "Groß ist die Diana"	Arie: "Fürchte dich nicht"	Choral: "O treuer Heiland"	[Rec.:] "Schnell aber"
	Alexander: "Alle Menschen sind Knechte"	Chor: "Fürchtet euch nicht"		Choral: "O treuer Heiland"
	Paulus: "Ich gebiete dir"			Arie: "So du mit deinem Mund bekennest"
	Die Herren: "Diese Menschen"			
	[Rec.:] "Und das Volk ward erreget"			
	[Rec.:] "Um die Mitternacht"			
	Paulus und Silas: "Gelobet sei Gott"			
	[Rec.:] "Schnell aber ward ein großes Erdbeben"			
	Paulus: "Thue dir nicht Übels"			
	Kerkermeister: "Liebe Herren, was soll ich thun"			
	Paulus und Silas: "Glaube an den Herrn"			
	Kerkermeister: "O wie ist die Barmherzigkeit"			

Continued on next page

(Table 5.8—Continued)

	Musical sources						
MN19	MN28	MN55ac	MN55pc	PS-NYPL	MN54	Program of premier	Simrock
							32. Rec.: "Und es war ein Mann zu Lystra"
	"No. 32 Chor"—"Danket den Göttern"	34. Rec.: "Da das aber die Heiden hörten . . . Und es war ein Mann zu Lystra"; Chor: "Die Götter sind den Menschen"	33. Rec.: "Da das aber die Heiden hörten . . . Und es war ein Mann zu Lystra"; Chor: "Die Götter sind den Menschen"	33. Rec.: "Da das aber die Heiden hörten . . . Und es war ein Mann zu Lystra"; Chor: "Die Götter sind den Menschen"	33. Rec.: "Da das aber die Heiden hörten . . . Und es war ein Mann zu Lystra"; Chor: "Die Götter sind den Menschen"	33. Rec.: "Da das aber die Heiden hörten . . . Und es war ein Mann zu Lystra"; Chor: "Die Götter sind den Menschen"	33. Coro: "Die Götter sind den Menschen"
		35. Rec.: "Und nannten Barnabas Jupiter"	34. Rec.: "Und nannten Barnabas Jupiter"	34. Rec.: "Und nannten Barnabas Jupiter"	34. Rec.: "Und nannten Barnabas Jupiter"	34. Rec.: "Und nannten Barnabas Jupiter"	34. Rec.: "Und nannten Barnabas Jupiter"
sketch: "Seid und gnädig"	[Chorus:] "Lobt ihn mit Pfeifen"	36. Chor: "Seid uns gnädig hohe Götter"	35. Chor: "Seid uns gnädig hohe Götter"	35. Chor: "Seid uns gnädig hohe Götter"	35. Chor: "Seid uns gnädig hohe Götter"	35. Chor: "Seid uns gnädig hohe Götter"	35. Coro: "Seid uns gnädig, hohe Götter"
[sketch:] "Danket dem Gott"	[Chorus:] "Danket dem Herrn"	36. cont. Rec.: "Da das die Apostel hörten"		36. Rec. [no music]	36. Rec.: "Da das die Apostel hörten"	36. Rec.: "Da das die Apostel hörten"	36. Rec.: "Da das die Apostel hörten"
		[37. Aria ending with:] ". . . Aber unser Gott ist im Himmel"		37. Arie [no music]	[37.] Arie: "Wisset ihr nicht"	37. Arie: "Wisset ihr nicht"	36. (cont.) Aria: "Wisset ihr nicht"
		38. Chor: "Aber unser Gott"	38. Chor: "Aber unser Gott"	38. Chor: "Aber unser Gott"	38. Chor: "Aber unser Gott"	38. Chor und Choral: "Aber unser Gott"	36. (cont.) Coro: "Aber unser Gott"
		39. Arioso: "Wisset ihr nicht"		39. Arioso [no music]			

Continued on next page

(Table 5.8—Continued)

MN19	MN28	MN55ac	MN55pc	PS-NYPL	MN54	Program of premier	Simrock
	"Gelobet sei Gott der Vater unseres Herrn", Rec.: "Schnell aber ward ein großes Erdbeben"	[39. cont.] Rec.: "Da ward das Volk erreget"	39. Rec.: "Da ward das Volk erreget"		39. Rec.: "Da ward das Volk erreget"	39. Rec.: "Da ward das Volk erreget"	37. Rec.: "Da ward das Volk erreget"
		40. Chor: "Hier ist des Herren Tempel"	40. Chor: "Hier ist des Herren Tempel"	40. Chor: "Hier ist des Herren Tempel"	40. Chor: "Hier ist des Herren Tempel"	40. Chor: "Hier ist des Herren Tempel"	38. Coro: "Hier ist des Herren Tempel"
		41. Rec.: "Und sie alle verfolgten Paulus"	41. Rec.: "Und sie alle verfolgten Paulus"; Cavatine "Sey getreu bis in den Tod"	41. Rec.: "Und alles Volk verfogte"	41. Rec.: "Und sie alle verfolgten Paulus"; Cavatine "Sey getreu bis in den Tod"	41. Rec.: "Und sie alle verfolgten Paulus"; Cavatine "Sey getreu bis in den Tod"	39. Rec.: "Und sie alle ver-folgten Paulus"
							40. Cavatina: "Sei getreu bis in den Tod"
	Choral: "O treuer Heiland Jesu Christ"	42. Choral: "Erhebe dich o meine Seel"	42. Choral: "Erhebe dich o meine Seel"	42. Choral: "Erhebe dich o meine Seel"	42. Choral: "Erhebe dich o meine Seel"	42. Choral: "Erhebe dich o meine Seel"	

Source. Sposato, Jeffrey, Mendelssohn's Theological Evolution: A Study of Textual Choice and Change in the Composer's Sacred Works.

Recitatives

The first recitative of scene 3 was revised before and after the first performance. Table 5.9 shows the revision stages of "Da das aber die Heiden hörten"/"Und es war ein Mann zu Lystra."

Table 5.9. Revision Stages of "Da das aber die Heiden hörten"/"Und es war ein Mann zu Lystra"

1. MN55ac

2. MN55pc

   PS-NYPL

3. MN54ac

4. MN54pc

5. Simrock

The most obvious revision of the opening recitative is the shortening of its text in the Simrock version (see Examples 5.10a-c). Mendelssohn completely eliminated the first sentence of MN54 and MN55, "Da das aber die Heiden hörten, wurden sie froh und priesen das Wort des Herrn" (Acts 13:48a). As seen in the transition from the first to the second scene, Mendelssohn's revision in the transition from the second to the third scene makes a clearer distinction between the scenes, since the discarded opening of the third scene belonged textually to the previous scene, which was based on Acts 13:45-48a.

A further comparison of the three versions of this recitative shows Mendelssohn's aim in his revisions to emphasize certain parts of the text. In the MN55 version the only words that are clearly emphasized are "Stehe auf." The revision in MN55 also emphasizes "und lobte Gott." Moreover, in the ensuing phrase in MN55 the name "Paulus" occurred on the downbeat of the measure, while in MN54 Mendelssohn changed this passage to have the word "Heiden" appear on the downbeat. This change in the music more accurately portrays the shift of focus in the action away from Paul toward the reaction of the Gentiles. The Simrock version keeps only the basic contours of this recitative. The most important revisions are rhythmic changes. Mendelssohn carefully controlled the rhythmic speed of the recitative. Whenever he wanted to emphasize important aspects of the text, he slowed the speed of the declamation; examples are Paul's call for healing starting on the

Example 5.10a. MN55, "Da das aber die Heiden"

Da das a-ber die Hei-den hör-ten wur-den sie froh und prie-sen das Wort des Herrn Und es

war ein Mann zu Ly-stra der war lahm und hat-te noch nie ge-wan-delt der hör-te Pau-lus re-den

und als er ihn an-sah sprach er mit lau-ter Stim-me Ste-he auf auf dei-ne

Fü-ße und er sprang auf und wan-del-te und lob-te Gott Da a-ber die Hei-den sa-hen was

Pau-lus ge-than ho-ben sie ih-re Stim-men auf und spra-chen zu-ein-an-der

Example 5.10b. MN54, "Da das aber die Heiden"

Da das a-ber die Hei-den hör-ten wur-den sie froh und prie-sen das Wort des Herrn Und es

war ein Mann zu Ly-stra der war lahm und hat-te noch nie ge-wan-delt der hör-te Pau-lus re-den

und als er ihn an-sah sprach er mit lau-ter Stim-me Ste-he auf auf dei-ne

Fü-ße und er sprang auf und wan-del-te und lob-te Gott Da a-ber die

Hei-den sa-hen was Pau-lus ge-than ho-ben sie ih-re Stim-men auf und spra-chen zu-ein-an-der

Example 5.10c Simrock, "Und es war ein Mann"

Und es war ein Mann zu Ly-stra, der war lahm und hat-te noch nie ge-wan-delt, der hör-te

Pau-lus re-den, und als er ihn an-sah, sprach er mit lau-ter Stim-me: Ste-he auf, auf dei-ne

Fü-ße! Und er sprang auf und wan-del-te und lo-be-te Gott. Da a-ber die

Hei-den sahn, was Pau-lus ge-than, ho-ben sie ih-re Stim-men auf und spra-chen zu-ein-an-der:

word "Stimme" and the reaction of the healed with the words "und lobete Gott." At the end of the recitative Mendelssohn prepared the ensuing turba chorus by increasing the speed of the syllables as the Gentiles react strongly to Paul's healing.

The second recitative, "Und nannten Barnabas Jupiter," does not show many revisions. While MN55 contains the earliest version of the recitative, it is nevertheless closer to the final version than to that of MN54. In MN54 Mendelssohn wanted to emphasize the frenzy of the previous chorus in contrast to the ensuing chorus of adoration. He retained the tenor from the previous recitative as the narrator rather than changing to soprano voice. In MN55 and in the Simrock version Mendelssohn assigned the recitative to the soprano, which helps to signal the change of mood from frenzy to adoration. Further, while in MN55 and the Simrock version the accompaniment consists of sustained chords, in MN54 Mendelssohn had changed some of the sustained chords to staccato interjections.

The third recitative, "Da das die Apostel hörten," and the ensuing aria following the second of the two *Heidenchöre* were rewritten twice. Table 5.10 shows the revision stages of "Da das die Apostel hörten."

Table 5.10. Revision Stages of "Da das die Apostel hörten"

1. MN55 (only the beginning is extant)
2. MN54ac
3. MN54pc
4. Simrock

Only MN54 still contains the complete old version of these two pieces. In MN55 Mendelssohn took out the folio containing most of these rejected movements. The remaining sections of these movements on the preceding and following bifolios are crossed out (see Figure 5.9). In PS-NYPL the copyist did not enter these movements but only wrote "No. 36 Recit.," and "No. 37 Arie" at the bottom of the last page of No. 35, "Seyd uns gnädig, hohe Götter." Mendelssohn must have already rejected the MN55 version by the time the copyist received the music. The version in MN54 probably reflects the version used in the first performance, after which Mendelssohn heavily revised it once again. He wrote to his mother on 16 August 1836,

Don't be angry with me because the piano-vocal score was delayed
so long; it was not my fault, it was Schleinitz the traitor, as Beckchen
will tell you, but this piano-vocal score is not the right one, the correct one will be printed in a few days. I would like best, therefore, if
you would not play through this incorrect one.[4]

A comparison of the openings of "Da das die Apostel" of MN55,
MN54, and the Simrock version shows why Mendelssohn decided to
rewrite this recitative. The MN55 version (Figure 5.9) seems unfocused
when compared to MN54 (see Example 5.11a). The opening measure
in MN55 does not have any melodic direction in the top line, because
the same pitch is repeated four times. In MN54 Mendelssohn changed
the top line to give it the needed intensity. The rhythmic emphases of
the text in MN55 do not stress important words. In MN54 Mendelssohn
changed the rhythm of the text, stressing "hörten" and "Kleider" as important words. In the Simrock version (see Example 5.11b) Mendelssohn augmented the rhythm of the instrumental opening, creating a less
frantic yet more theatrical beginning of the recitative. The change with
the most impact continues to be found in the instrumental parts. Although in MN54 the winds enter on the words "und sprachen" to show
Paul's fury, in the later Simrock version Mendelssohn did not use
winds at all. This changes the character of Paul's reaction tremendously, making him now seem less angry. At the same time Mendelssohn focused more on the content of the words. After the words "Wir
sind auch sterbliche Menschen wie ihr" he used the same musical figure as before for a third time, yet he altered it, using an augmented second (Example 5.11b, mm. 13, 14), to emphasize the word "sterbliche."
By reducing the instrumental forces, Mendelssohn did not make the
recitative less effective; rather, he changed the character of the response, making Paul seem less furious.

Aria

The aria "Wisset ihr nicht" first appears in MN55. As Table 5.8
shows, its original location in this scene was after the chorus "Aber unser Gott" rather than before. By moving the aria in front of the chorus,
Mendelssohn made the scene more dramatic, placing the large chorus,
rather than the aria, immediately before the hostile reaction of the Gen-
tile crowd. Mendelssohn did not merely change the location of the aria,
however. He crossed out the aria completely in order to write a new
one, which he then placed in front of the chorus. Mendelssohn was not
satisfied with the replacement aria of MN54 either; after the first performance of *Paulus* he almost completely rewrote the aria once again.

Figure 5.9. MN55, p. 73v.

Mendelssohn titled the MN55 version of "Wisset ihr nicht" *Arioso*, which describes this movement accurately. It is a simple, short setting of the text with plain accompaniment (see Example 5.12a). MN54 contains a much more expressive presentation of the text. While the fury of the preceding recitative is no longer present, the accompaniment makes Paul's sermon to the Gentiles seem harsher than it later became in the

Example 5.11a. MN54, "Da das die Apostel hörten"

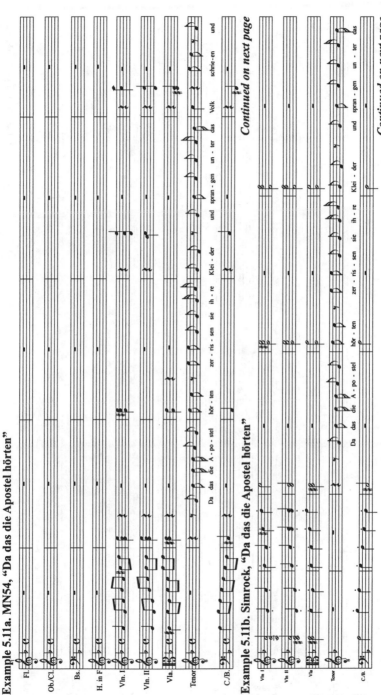

Continued on next page

Example 5.11b. Simrock, "Da das die Apostel hörten"

Continued on next page

(Example 5.11a—Continued)

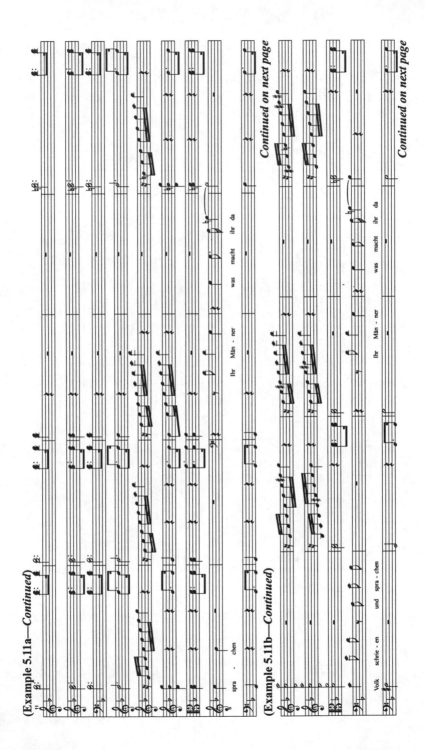

Continued on next page

(Example 5.11b—Continued)

Continued on next page

(Example 5.11a—*Continued*)

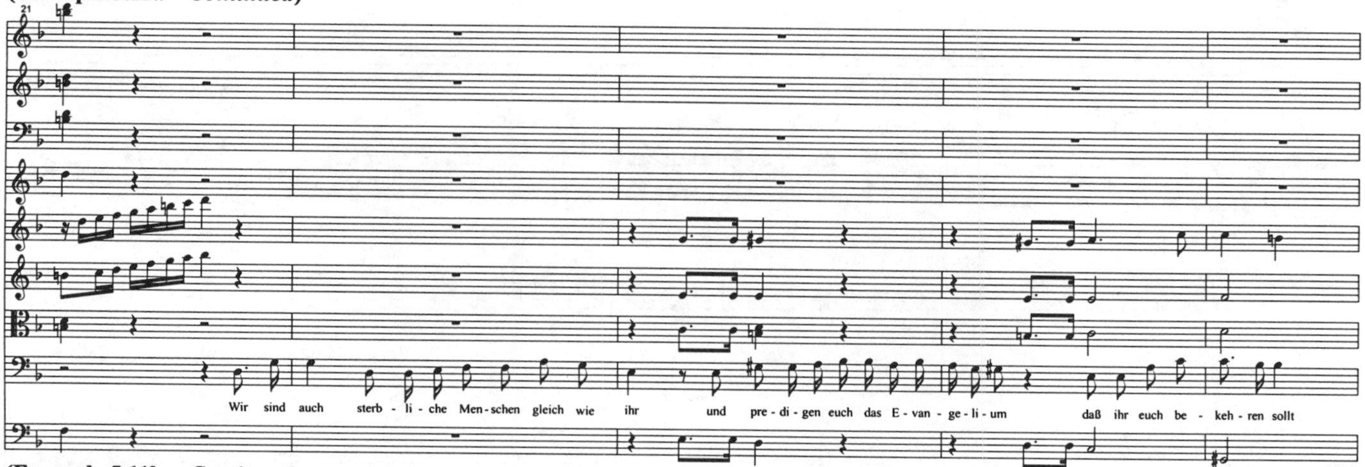

(Example 5.11b—*Continued*)

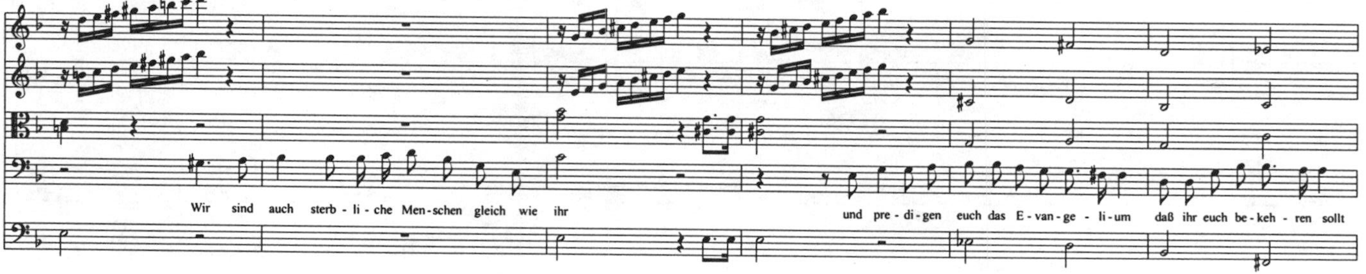

Example 5.12a. MN55, "Wisset ihr nicht"

Wis-set ihr nicht daß ihr Got-tes Tem-pel seid und der Geist Got-tes in euch woh - net

Example 5.12b. MN54, "Wisset ihr nicht"

Wis - set ihr nicht daß ihr Got-tes Tem - pel seid und daß der Geist Got-tes in euch woh-net

Example 5.12c. Simrock, "Wisset ihr nicht"

final version (compare Examples 5.12b and c). The Simrock version is also twenty-three measures longer than the MN54 version. Its main focus is on the good news of the gospel rather than on its harshness, which is more emphasized in MN54. While in MN54 the last part of the aria on the text "Denn der Tempel Gottes ist heilig, der seid ihr" is only twelve measures long, the same text in the Simrock version makes for a twenty-five-measure section.

Choruses

Of the three choruses that are contained in the published version, two are the so-called *Heidenchöre*. The first one, "Die Götter sind den Menschen," represents an excited, frantic crowd, while the second chorus, "Seid uns gnädig," is prayerful. Neither chorus shows many revisions. The third chorus, "Aber unser Gott," however, was heavily revised.

"Die Götter sind den Menschen" shows only ten revisions. Most of them are minute voice-leading adjustments. The most extensive revision is found in mm. 17-25 (see Examples 5.13a-c). In the first version, found in MN55 (Example 5.13a), Mendelssohn set the first part of the phrase in unison. In his first revision he moved away from the unison (see Example 5.13b), retaining the previous unison version as the bass line.

In the printed version Mendelssohn decided that, while he did not want unison sound, he wanted a simpler phrase, which would fit better in this turba choir (see Example 5.13c).

"Seid uns gnädig" shows mainly the same revisions of detail as "Die Götter sind." The only somewhat substantial changes are found in the instrumentation. While in MN54 the clarinets double the vocal part and the violas from the very beginning, in the Simrock version Mendelssohn delayed the entrances of clarinets by ten measures, creating a stronger intensification effect with the choral entrances. Mendelssohn made a corresponding instrumental revision again later in the piece, where he delayed the entrance of the oboes in the Simrock version. MN19 contains a brief sketch of the opening theme of "Seid und gnädig."

MN28 contains three more, rejected *Heidenchöre*, "Danket den Göttern," "Lobt ihn mit Pfeifen," and "Danket dem Herrn." The text and probable placement of all three choruses is clarified by the c. 27 drafts (see Table 5.8). The first of these three rejected choruses, "Danket den Göttern," is headed "No. 32 Chor." The fact that it was numbered suggests that it was taken out rather late in the revision process, since Mendelssohn did not number the movements until late in the

Example 5.13a. MN55, "Die Götter sind den Menschen"

Example 5.13b. MN54, "Die Götter sind den Menschen"

Example 5.13c. Simrock, "Die Götter sind den Menschen"

process. It was, however, never part of one of the last versions either, for its numbering is two numbers too low to be placed in MN54. Since the chorus does not show many revisions, it might be assumed that this is not the first copy of the movement. Only once did Mendelssohn cut three measures (at the end of a transitional section, which is typical for Mendelssohn's tightening of the movements); all of the other revisions are small voice-leading or textual adjustments. The question as to why

Mendelssohn cut this chorus can be answered by its function in this scene, or rather its lack thereof. It does not add any new aspect that the preceding chorus and the following recitative do not express. It would have been merely an unnecessary prolongation of the deification of Paul and Barnabas. Possibly Mendelssohn thought that the emphasis on the deification might undermine and weaken the more important aspect of this scene, Paul's presentation of the gospel.

The second and third of the *Heidenchöre* of MN28 were probably supposed to appear side by side, as c.27 suggests (see Table 5.8). "Lobt ihn mit Pfeifen" shows evidence that it was originally placed right after the chorus "Seid uns gnädig." It contains the last chord of the preceding movement, an A-major chord with the syllable "-fer." Since "Seid uns gnädig" is in A major, and because its last word is "Opfer," it seems reasonable to assume that this last chord belongs to an earlier version of "Seid uns gnädig" (none of the extant versions of "Seid uns gnädig" actually ends on exactly that chord). "Lobt ihn mit Pfeifen" is the longest of all the *Heidenchöre*; it is 223 measures and 28 pages long. In a letter written on Christmas day in 1834 Mendelssohn mentioned the composing of a chorus in F-sharp minor—"Lobt ihn mit Pfeifen" is the only chorus in that key—in a letter to Moscheles:

> My Oratorio is making great progress. I am working at the second part, and have just written a Chorus in F sharp minor (a lively chorus of heathens) which I thoroughly relish myself and should so much like to show you; in fact, I am ever so anxious to hear whether you are satisfied with my new work.[5]

MN19 contains a one-line continuity draft of "Lobt ihn mit Pfeifen." Except for the main themes, however, the continuity draft is completely different from the later, scored version.

Following "Lobt ihn mit Pfeifen" is the two-part women's chorus "Danket dem Herrn." A short, slow tenor introduction serves as transition from the F-sharp minor of the previous chorus to the G major of "Danket dem Herrn." The MN28 version once again appears to be a revised version, since it is cleanly written and contains virtually no revisions. The rejection of these choruses seems textually and dramaturgically, rather than musically, motivated. As was the case with "Danket den Göttern," these choruses do not convey any new content. Their length hinders rather than furthers the dramatic flow of this scene. They furthermore undermine Paul's and Barnabas's surprised and immediate response to their deification. As Michael Cooper also points out, "Danket dem Herrn," does not fit well textually, since it refers to one God only.[6] MN19 contains a short thematic sketch using the words "Danket dem Gott, dem Gott aller Götter," which might have been an initial idea for a chorus for this scene. It is not related musically to "Danket dem Herrn" of MN28.

The cutting of the three *Heidenchöre* of MN28 was also encouraged by Schubring in a letter from 6 October 1835:

> At the place of the heathen offering in Lystra it has become more and more obvious to me that it is too long after all. In such an oratorio one could show the darkness of paganism in order to let the gospel illuminate the darkness through the apostle to the Gentiles (like the aria in B minor in *Messiah*, "The people that walked in darkness . . ."). That is not the case in these choruses, however; after this situation there perhaps ought to be some sumptuous music during this idolatry, which for this oratorio might be too dramatic. Therefore I now believe you would do best just to have a ritornello . . . played here, which Paul then interrupts.[7]

Mendelssohn not only cut three *Heidenchöre*, he also took up Schubring's idea of Paul interrupting the idolatry—displayed by the chorus "Seid uns gnädig"—with the recitative, "Da das die Apostel hörten." Note that the rejected movements were written on paper of type A, while the new movements were written on paper type C, establishing the paper type A as the earliest paper type and paper type C as the next paper type used.

The third chorus of the published version, "Aber unser Gott," which is not a *Heidenchor*, shows a different revision pattern than the other two movements in this first part of scene 3. Table 5.11 shows the revision stages of "Aber unser Gott."

Table 5.11. Revision Stages of "Aber unser Gott"

1. MN54ac
2a. MN54pc
2b. PS-NYPL
MN55
Simrock

MN54 contains the earliest extant version of this chorus and shows substantial revisions. MN55 and the Simrock version are clean copies of the revised MN54 version. PS-NYPL contains a version almost identical to that of MN55 and the Simrock version; the soprano line is different in one passage.

Contrapuntally, this is the most complex movement of *Paulus*. It is a double fugue that incorporates the first part of the Lutheran chorale "Wir glauben all an einen Gott" as cantus firmus. Not surprisingly, most revisions are structural ones. Mendelssohn crossed out twenty-four measures in MN54. Mendelssohn's aim in his revisions was a more symmetrical positioning of the cantus firmus. Most of the contrapuntal revisions are adjustments to accommodate the cuts. Another important revision concerning the chorale is the use of the text. While in all the sources before the first performance the chorale was played by instruments, in the Simrock version Mendelssohn decided to have the cantus firmus also sung by the second sopranos, which obviously places more emphasis on the chorale.

The Gentiles Reject Paul's Message

Introduction

Although the first part of this scene was heavily revised, the second part does not show quite as many revisions; most of the revisions were made before the first performance. The order of the sources in the revision process is the same throughout the scene. MN55 contains the earliest version, and PS-NYPL is a clean copy of MN55; MN54 contains the next layers of revision; the Simrock version is mostly identical with MN54. MN28 contains the rejected movements of the previously planned prison scene. These three movements appear in the order of the c. 27 draft, indicating that Mendelssohn deleted this scene, replacing it with the recitative "Und sie verfolgten" and the cavatina "Sei getreu bis in den Tod." This replacement is understandable, since the prison scene displays God's power, which has already been demonstrated in scene 3, while the new ending focuses on a new plot element.

Recitatives

There are only two short recitatives in this section of scene 3. Table 5.12 shows the revision stages of "Da ward das Volk." As discussed previously, in MN55 the aria "Wisset ihr nicht" was placed directly before the first recitative. While Mendelssohn crossed out the aria and replaced it with a new setting, the recitative needed few revisions and

Table 5.12. Revision Stages of "Da ward das Volk"

1. MN55ac
2. MN55pc
PS-NYPL
3. MN54ac
4. MN54pc
5. Simrock

was therefore not crossed out. A comparison of MN55ac with MN54pc/Simrock (Examples 5.14a and b) shows the revised version as more exciting, expressing the intensity of the words better through the placement of the chords on offbeats (mm. 1, 4), the more frequent use of seventh chords (mm. 1, 4), as well as larger melodic leaps (mm. 3, 4, and 7).

The revision stages of the second recitative, "Und sie alle verfolgten Paulus," are very similar to those in the first recitative. This second recitative does not appear yet in PS-NYPL. At the time PS-NYPL was produced, Mendelssohn must already have planned to revise the second recitative, and he did not want the copyist to include the unrevised version. Most of the changes in the second recitative are found in the vocal line (see Examples 5.15a and b). As portrayed in the first recitative, "Und sie alle verfolgten" also shows changes that emphasize important words and phrases more effectively. The word "stärkte" is emphasized in this context rather than "Herr," and the phrase "und alle Heiden hörten" is portrayed stronger in MN54.

Chorus

There is only one chorus in this section, "Hier ist des Herren Tempel." It is another turba choir, representing angry Jews as well as Gentiles. Table 5.13 shows the revision stages of this chorus. Even though two layers of revision are found in MN55, the changes are not substantial. The first round of revisions was notated in ink, consisting of small text adjustments and some chords that were rescored to place the pitches in the lower range of the vocal parts. The second round of revisions was entered in pencil, making a few more of the same types of adjustments. PS-NYPL is a clean copy of the revised version. MN54 shows revisions only in the orchestration. Interestingly enough, some of those also were written in pencil, while most are in ink. It seems that

Example 5.14a. MN55, "Da ward das Volk"

Example 5.14b. MN54/Simrock, "Da ward das Volk"

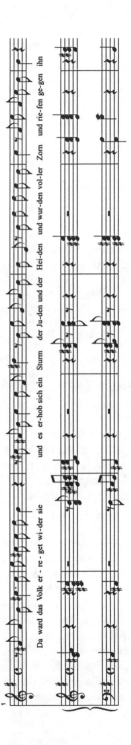

Example 5.15a. MN55, "Und alles Volk verfolgte"

Example 5.15b. MN54, "Und sie alle verfolgten"

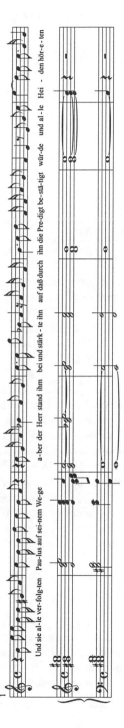

Table 5.13. Revision Stages of "Hier ist des Herren Tempel"

1. MN55I
2. MN55II
3. MN55III
4. MN54I
PS-NYPL
5. MN54II
6. MN54III
7. Simrock

Mendelssohn used pencil in more than one revision process, because some of the earlier revisions of this movement in MN55 also were in pencil.

The revisions in instrumentation continue and are even more extensive during the last revision process, leading up to the Simrock version. In the opening measures in MN54 the choir started a cappella, while in the Simrock version Mendelssohn doubled the choir with the strings. On several occasions later on in the movement Mendelssohn cut instrumental parts that were not just doubling the vocal parts. The result of these changes is a powerful-sounding choir, portraying the angry crowd more effectively. The only noteworthy changes in the vocal parts are found toward the end of the movement at the words "Steiniget ihn" (see Examples 5.16a and b). The music brings back motives from a turba choir of the first part of the oratorio. While the earlier, MN54, version uses both main motives of the reused section of the first part, "Steiniget ihn" and "er lästert Gott," the Simrock version uses only the "Steiniget ihn" motive. Only once in the Simrock version, in m. 45 in the bass, do the words "er lästert ihn" occur. Since this is the only time that this movement uses these words, one has to wonder if this occurrence slipped past the composer in the final revision process.

Cavatina

The cavatina may have been the last movement added to this scene, since it does not appear in PS-NYPL. While there are other movements not actually present in the piano-vocal score, all the other missing movements are nevertheless listed as movements to be added. PS-NYPL, however, makes no mention of the cavatina. "Sei getreu bis

Example 5.16a. MN54, "Hier ist des Herren Tempel"

Continued on next page

Example 5.16b. Simrock, "Hier ist des Herren Tempel"

Continued on next page

(Example 5.16a—*Continued*)

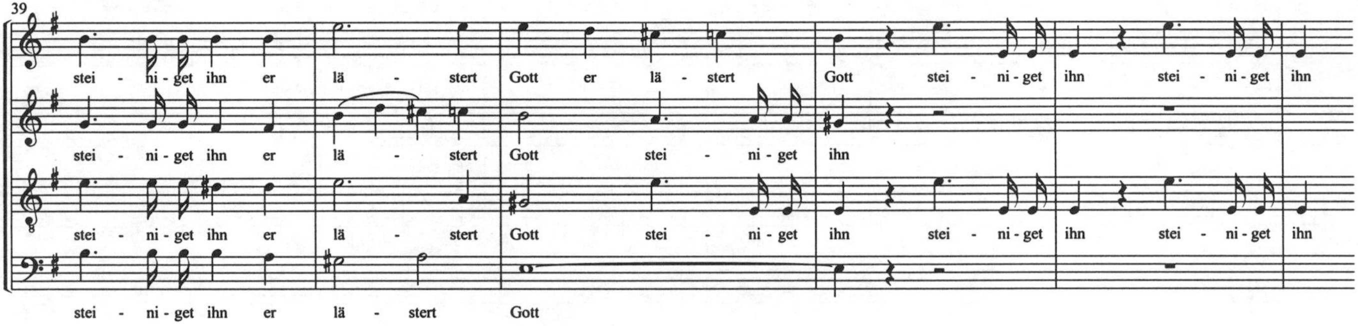

(Example 5.16b—*Continued*)

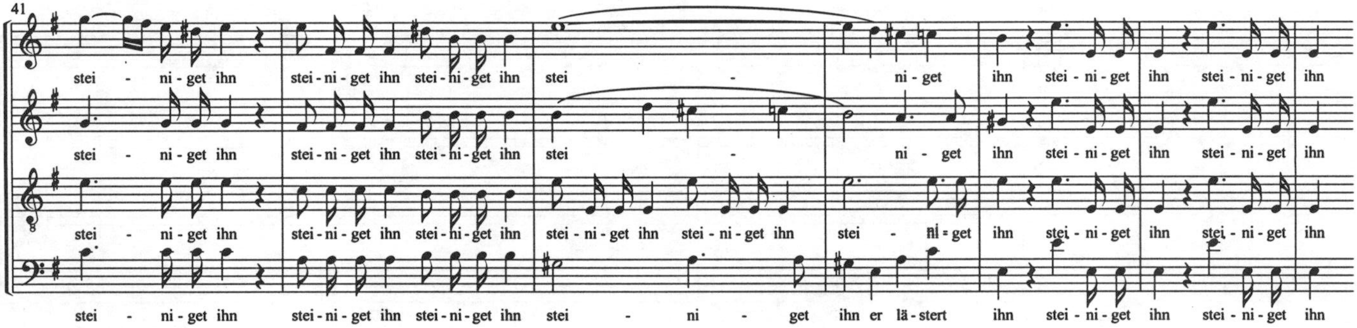

in den Tod" was inserted clearly into MN55. It appears by itself on a bifolio of which the last page is empty. At the top of the bifolio containing the cavatina Mendelssohn wrote the customary initials for a first draft, "H. d. m." ("hilf du mir"), which indicates that this is the first complete draft of the cavatina. It is surprising then, that the cavatina was hardly revised. MN55 only contains two revisions, one pitch change and one word change.

The revisions in MN54 are not very extensive. The most substantial changes are found at the end of the opening section (see Examples 5.17a and b). As shown in the recitatives, here also Mendelssohn moved the important words to the beginnings of measures. In addition, by raising the vocal line an octave in m. 12, Mendelssohn created a more effective phrase ending.

Example 5.17a. MN55, "Sei getreu bis in den Tod"

Example 5.17b. MN54, "Sei getreu bis in den Tod"

Chorale

Except for a few minute changes, the chorale, "Erhebe dich o meine Seele," was not revised. While it appears in all the complete manuscripts, it was cut after the premiere. Mendelssohn might have felt that the cavatina "Sei getreu bis in den Tod" already provided the reflective moment desired at that point.

Paul's Farewell

Overview

This last scene shows the same revision process as the previous one; it, likewise, was heavily revised before and after the first performance. The recitatives and the *Schlußchor* show the most substantial changes. Table 5.14 shows the drafts for this scene.

Recitatives

There are four different versions of the opening recitative, "Paulus sandte hin." Table 5.15 shows its revision stages.

Table 5.15. Revision Stages of "Paulus sandte hin"

1. MN28
2. MN55ac
3. MN55pc
PS-NYPL
4. MN54ac
5. MN54pc
6. Simrock

While the overall structure is the same in all four versions, many smaller revisions are found. The MN28 version is the least similar to the other three versions. Examples 5.18a-d show the openings of the different versions of the recitative. The revisions show Mendelssohn's concern with the expression of the vocal line as the most important aspect. He simplified the accompaniment after Example 5.18a, making the recitation of the text the main expressive element. Examples 5.18b-d exemplify the cautious and tedious revision process in which Mendelssohn tried out other possibilities (Example 5.18c), before settling on a modified earlier version (Examples 5.18b and 5.18d).

There are only three different versions of the second recitative, because MN28 does not contain any other recitatives for this scene. While

Table 5.14. Sources of Part 2, Scene 4

	Libretto sources				
FMB—MDM c.42	Fürst—d. 53, no. 87; d. 30, no. 211	Marx—d. 53, no. 88	FMB—d.30, no. 211; Schubring's comments	FMB—c. 27, p. 28r-30v	FMB—c. 27, p. 31r-32r
from Acts 20:16-35 [Denn Paulus hatte beschlossen] Die Jünger wollen ihn zurück halten	[Rec.:] "Paulus eilete auf den Pfingsttag"	[Rec.:] "Und stärkete sich im Glauben"	[Rec.:] "Paulus sandte hin und ließ fordern"	[Rec.:] "Paulus sandte hin und ließ fordern"	[Rec.:] "Paulus sandte hin p.p."
Paulus: Acts 6:10 [Zuletzt, meine Brüder]	Paulus: "Siehe, ich bin im Geiste"	Paulus: "Siehe, ich bin im Geiste"	Chor: "O schone doch deiner selbst"	Chor: "O schone doch deiner selbst"	Chor: "Schone doch deiner selbst"
Acts 20:28; 1. Co. 2:4-6, 4:1, 12:12, 13:1; 2. Co. 2:24, 3:6, 3:17,7:23; Eph. 2:19; Gal. 2:20, 3:21-24, 6:15	Jünger: "Herr, schone doch deiner selbst"	Rec.: "es ward aber viel Weinens"	Paulus: "Was machet ihr daß ihr weinet"	Paulus: "Was machet ihr daß ihr weinet"	Chor: "Des Herr Wille geschehe"
	Andere: "Das widerfahre dir nur nicht"	Paulus: "Was machet ihr daß ihr weinet"	Chor: "Des Herr Wille geschehe"/ "Der Herr aber wird mich erlösen"	Chor: "Des Herr Wille geschehe"/ "Der Herr aber wird mich von allem Übels"	[Rec.:] "Darum seid wacher"
Jünger: Rom. 15:31; Mt. 26:39	Arie oder Duet: "Meine Augen müssen mit Thränen"	[Rec.:] "Da sprachen alle, des Herrn Wille geschehe"	Paulus: "Und ob ich geopfert werde"	Chor: "Ziehe hin mit Frieden"	Chor: "Ziehe hin. Gott sei mit dir"
"Und Paulus zog hinauf gen Jerusalem"	Paulus: "Was machet ihr da ihr weinet"	Paulus: "Du bist der Herr"	Chor: "Wir leben oder sterben"	Chor: "Jesus Christus gestern und heute"	Chor: "Er hat einen guten Kampf gekämpft"
2. Tim. 4:7-8, "Er hat [einen guten Kampf gekämpft]" Schluchor	Jünger: "Des Herrn Wille geschehe" Paulus: "Das weiß ich"	Schlußchor mit Paulus: "Wer will uns scheiden"		[Rec.:] "Das weiß ich"	Chor: "Denn aber der Überschwängliches"
	Arie: "Wenn ich mit Menschen und Engelzunge"			Arie: "Ziehe hin mit Frieden"	
				Chor: "Er hat einen guten Kampf gekämpft"	

Continued on next page

(Table 5.14—*Continued*)

		Musical sources				
MN19	MN28	MN55	PS-NYPL	MN54	Program of premier	Simrock
"Schone doch deiner selbst"	Rec.: "Paulus sandte hin und ließ fordern die Ältesten"	43. Rec.: "Paulus sandte hin und ließ fordern die Ältesten" [43. cont.] Chor: "Schone doch deiner selbst"; Paulus: "Was machet ihr"; Chor: "Des Herrn Wille geschehe"; Rec.: "Und als er das gesagt" 44. Chor: "Sehet, welch eine Liebe" 45. Rec.: "Und wenn er schon geopfert wird" 46. Schlußchor: "Nicht aber ihm sondern allen"	43. Rec.: "Paulus sandte hin und ließ fordern die Ältesten" [43. cont.] Chor: "Schone doch deiner selbst"; Paulus: "Was machet ihr"; Chor: "Des Herrn Wille geschehe"; Rec.: "Und als er das gesagt" 44. Chor: "Sehet, welch eine Liebe" 45. Rec.: "Und wenn er schon geopfert wird" 46. Schlußchor: "Nicht aber ihm sondern allen"	43. Rec.: "Paulus sandte hin und ließ fordern die Ältesten" [43. cont.] Chor: "Schone doch deiner selbst"; Paulus: "Was machet ihr"; Chor: "Des Herrn Wille geschehe"; Rec.: "Und als er das gesagt" 44. Chor: "Sehet, welch eine Liebe" 45. Rec.: "Und wenn er schon geopfert wird" 46. Schlußchor: "Nicht aber ihm sondern allen"	43. Rec.: "Paulus sandte hin und ließ fordern die Ältesten" [43. cont.] Chor: "Schone doch deiner selbst"; Paulus: "Was machet ihr"; Chor: "Des Herrn Wille geschehe"; Rec.: "Und als er das gesagt" 44. Chor: "Sehet, welch eine Liebe" 45. Rec.: "Und wenn er schon geopfert wird" 46. Schlußchor: "Nicht aber ihm sondern allen"	43. Rec.: "Paulus sandte hin und ließ fordern die Ältesten" 42. Coro: "Schone doch deiner selbst"; Rec.: "Was machet ihr" 43. Coro: "Sehet, welch eine Liebe" 44. Rec.: "Und wenn er schon geopfert wird" 45. Schlußchor: "Nicht aber ihm sondern allen"

Source. Sposato, Jeffrey, *Mendelssohn's Theological Evolution: A Study of Textual Choice and Change in the Composer's Sacred Works.*

Example 5.18a. MN28, "Paulus sandte hin"

Continued on next page

Example 5.18b. MN55, "Paulus sandte hin"

Continued on next page

Example 5.18c. MN54, "Paulus sandte hin"

Continued on next page

Example 5.18d. Simrock, "Paulus sandte hin"

Continued on next page

(Example 5.18a—*Continued*)

(Example 5.18b—*Continued*)

(Example 5.18c—*Continued*)

(Example 5.18d—*Continued*)

MN54 gives only a revised version of MN55, the Simrock version is also different structurally. The MN55/MN54 versions contain a brief chorus on the words "Des Herrn Wille geschehe, gelobet sey der Herr"; in the Simrock version Mendelssohn cut the chorus. By taking out the chorus, he moved the action along more quickly, which he thought necessary in this reflective farewell scene. More evidence for his intention can be found in another textual cut he made in this recitative. Mendelssohn also cut the section starting with "Und ob ich schon geopfert werde. . . ." This text is somewhat redundant with the third recitative, "Und wenn er schon geopfert wird." A comparison of these three versions shows revisions to the vocal part and to the accompaniment (see Examples 5.19a-c). The MN55 and MN54 versions are very similar; MN54 intensifies Paul's strong response through a more active accompaniment (m. 2) and a rhythmically better text declamation. The Simrock version, however, softens Paul's response through melodic, rhythmic, and harmonic revisions, making it seem caring rather than harsh. As in the deification scene, where Mendelssohn changed the portrayal of Paul to show the apostle as a gentler person, here also he brings out Paul's gentleness.

The last recitative, "Und wenn er gleich geopfert," continues Mendelssohn's interpretive changes seen before. A comparison of the MN55 version with the Simrock version shows a completely different musical interpretation of the text. Even though the vocal lines of these two versions are similar, the accompaniments are completely different. While the instrumental part of MN55 emphasizes the heroism of Paul, the instruments of the published version function as chordal recitative accompaniment (see Examples 5.20a and b). MN54 contains a revised version of MN55.

Choruses

Besides the ejected, short chorus in the first recitative of the last scene, there are three more choruses; "Schone doch deiner selbst" is the shortest of them. Few revisions were made in this chorus. Besides a handful of note and syllable adjustments, the only other revisions is a cut of two measures in MN55, which contains the earliest complete version. As with most of Mendelssohn's cuts, this one also happens toward the end of a phrase; the cut gives the phrase stronger direction toward the cadence. MN19 contains a short draft of the opening of this chorus, written in piano score (see Example 5.21), in which the only similarities to any later version are the two main themes.

Example 5.19a. MN55, "Was machet ihr, daß ihr weinet"

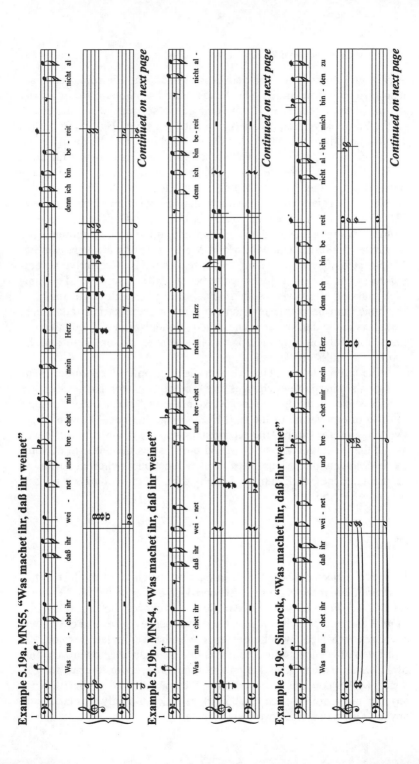

Continued on next page

Example 5.19b. MN54, "Was machet ihr, daß ihr weinet"

Continued on next page

Example 5.19c. Simrock, "Was machet ihr, daß ihr weinet"

Continued on next page

(Example 5.19a—*Continued*)

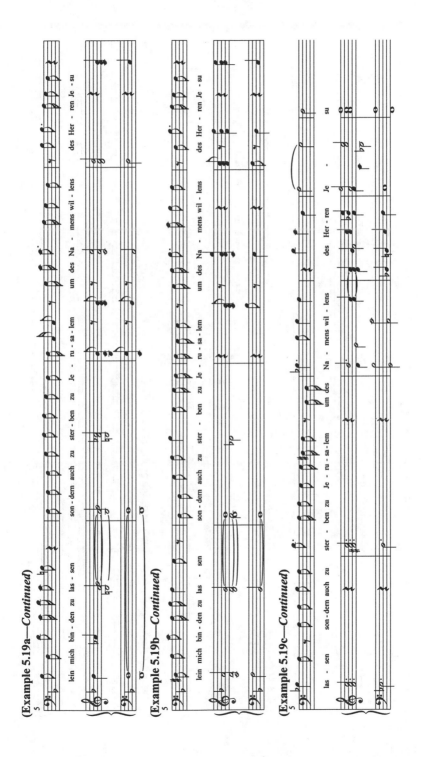

(Example 5.19b—*Continued*)

(Example 5.19c—*Continued*)

Example 5.20a. MN55, "Und wenn er schon geopfert wird"

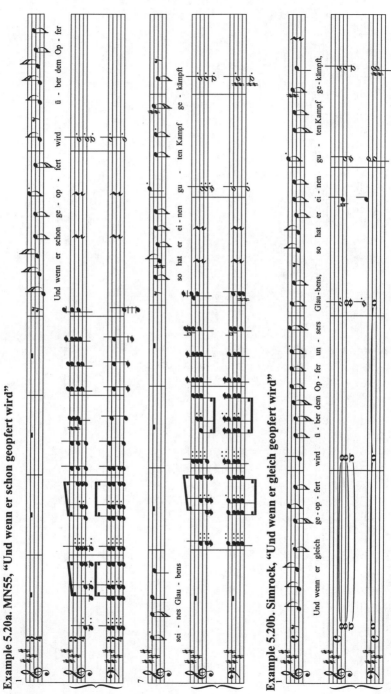

Example 5.20b. Simrock, "Und wenn er gleich geopfert wird"

Example 5.21. MN19, Sketch of "Schone doch deiner selbst"

The second chorus, "Sehet welch eine Liebe," shows only a few more revisions than the first one. There is also a two-measure cut, serving the same purpose as the cut in "Schone doch deiner selbst." The only other substantial changes are at the beginning of an imitative setting of the second part of the text, "daß wir Gottes Kinder sollen heißen" (see Examples 5.22a and b). In the Simrock version Mendelssohn delayed the bass entrance in order to have all entrances evenly spaced. He made all the necessary harmonic and contrapuntal adjustments to make the imitation most effective with pairs of entrances a fifth apart (c-g, f-b^b).

Although there were few revisions in the two earlier choruses of this last scene, the *Schlußchor* shows heavy revisions. The numerous

Example 5.22a. MN55, "Sehet welch eine Liebe"

Example 5.22b. Simrock, "Sehet welch eine Liebe"

changes throughout the movement date from both before and after the first performance. MN55 contains the earliest version with numerous changes; MN54 contains a much cleaner score, which matches the corrected MN55 version. The changes found in MN55 are typical contrapuntal revisions comparable to those effected in earlier movements. Mendelssohn also crossed out eleven measures, tightening the structure of the second part of this *Schlußchor*, which is a double fugue.

The more striking revisions took place after the first performance. Mendelssohn wrote to his mother on 20 August 1836,

> a few days ago I finished the last work on my oratorio, in which I finished a new and, it seems to me, much improved *Schlußchor*. And strangely, on the day I wrote the last note, the English publisher, who had traveled to Bonn to pick up the full score, arrived here, since Sir George Smart did not want to agree to a performance otherwise. Here he found the *Schlußchor* completed, and traveled back very satisfied.[8]

The first part of this long chorus, "Nicht aber ihm allein," shows some important conceptual changes. While the *maestoso* style of the earlier versions is expressed through tied-over triplets, Mendelssohn changed these triplet figures to dotted quarter/sixteenth-note figures, giving the opening a more fanfare-like character (see Examples 5.23a and b).

Example 5.23a. MN54, "Nicht aber ihm allein" I

Example 5.23b. Simrock, "Nicht aber ihm allein" I

There are also some unusual structural revisions in this opening section. In a move quite atypical of his correction process Mendelssohn actually added measures rather than cut them. He inserted eight measures toward the end of this opening section, effecting a broader ending.

The second, longer part is a double fugue, which Mendelssohn reworked, as he did in the opening section. Both fugue themes were carefully rewritten, which then became the basis for his contrapuntal revisions. Comparison of the exposition of the first fugue theme before and after the changes shows a more flowing revised theme (see Examples 5.24a and b); its revisions have obvious harmonic implications for the counterpoint of the whole fugue. A comparison of the *ante-* and *post-correcturam* expositions of the second fugue displays the improvements of the revised version very well (see Examples 5.25a and b). The earlier version uses only short motives of the first theme throughout the exposition, obscuring the second theme's entrances. In the Simrock version Mendelssohn adjusted the second theme in order to use the first theme as a counterpoint. By placing the first theme in the instrumental parts, he was able to tighten the double fugue's structure and at the same time have a more precise exposition of the second theme. The tenor entrance in the Simrock version (m. 90) completes the pattern of entrances on successive fifths (c#-f#-b-e), which was not the case in the MN54 version (m.83; c#-f#-b-d).

Example 5.24a. MN54, "Nicht aber ihm allein" II

Example 5.24b. Simrock, "Nicht aber ihm" II

Example 5.25a. MN54, "Nicht aber ihm allein" III

Example 5.25b. Simrock, "Nicht aber ihm allein" III

Notes

1. Erich Reimer, "Mendelssohns 'edler Gesang': Zur Kompositionsweise der Sologesänge im Paulus," *Archiv für Musikwissenschaft* 50/1 (1993): 60.

2. Felix Mendelssohn, Leipzig, to Ferdinand von Woringen, Düsseldorf, ALS, 21 April 1836, Heinrich-Heine-Institut Düsseldorf, Musikvereinsdepos. letter 15: Hierbei erfolgt der Rest des zweiten Theiles meiner Partitur. Ich bitte sie dem Abschreiber sofort zuzustellen, und ihm zu sagen, daß die Aria welche nach dem Recitativ No. 32 folgen soll, eingelegt werden muß, ebenso wie eine andre Arie, welche nach No. 30 folgen soll. Ich werde diese beiden Arien selbst erst mitbringen, und sie können dann erst ausgeschrieben und in die Nummern geheftet werden. Er muß sich bei der Arbeit sehr in acht nehmen, da die Partitur weniger, als gut geschrieben ist; am besten wäre es, wie ich schon früher schrieb, wenn Schauseil, falls er noch in Düsseldorf ist, die Stimmen auszöge.

3. See note 101.

4. Felix Mendelssohn, Frankfurt, to his mother, Berlin, ALS, 16 August 1836, New York Public Library: Sey mir nicht böse, daß der Clavierauszug so lange ausblieb, ich konnte nicht dafür sondern Schleinitz der Verräther, wie Beckchen dir sagen wird; aber dieser Clav. Ausz. ist gar nicht der rechte, sondern der rechte wird erst in einigen Tagen gedruckt kommen, drum wär mirs am liebsten, du spielest den falschen gar nicht erst durch.

5. Felix Mendelssohn, *Letters of Felix Mendelssohn to Ignaz and Charlotte Moscheles*, ed. and trans. by Felix Moscheles (Boston, Ticknor, 1888), 121.

6. Personal correspondence with John Michael Cooper.

7. Felix Mendelssohn, *Briefwechsel zwischen Felix Mendelssohn und J. Schubring zugleich ein Beitrag zur Geschichte des Oratoriums*, 96: Bei dem Heidenopfer in Lystra ist es immer fühlbarer geworden, daß das doch zu lang ist. Man könnte wohl in solch einem Oratorium die Finsternisse des Heidenthums angeben, um nachher das Evangelium durch den Heidenapostel hineinscheinen zu lassen (wie die Arie im Messias aus h-moll: das Volk so im Finstern wandelt u.s.w.). Aber das liegt in diesen Chören nicht; nach der Situation müßte vielleicht eine sinnlich üppige oder dergleichen Musik beim Götzendienst vorkommen, was wieder für das Oratorium zu dramatisch würde. Daher glaube ich jetzt, du würdest am besten thun, nach dem ersten Chor höchstens noch ein Ritornell . . . spielen zu lassen, so daß dann schon Paulus unterbrechend hineinfährt.

8. Felix Mendelssohn, Frankfurt, to his mother, Berlin, ALS, 20 August 1836, New York Public Library: . . . vor einigen Tagen habe ich dann auch die letzte Arbeit an meinem Oratorium beendigt, in dem ich einen neuen, und wie mir scheint viel besseren Schlußchor fertig gemacht habe. Und sonderbar an dem Tage, wo ich die letzte Note schrieb, kam der englische Verleger hier an, der nach Bonn gereist war, um sich die Partitur zu holen, weil Sir George Smart sonst nicht die Aufführung willigen wollte. Hier fand er auch den Schlußchor fertig, und reiste sehr zufrieden wieder zurück.

Chapter 6

Principles Governing the
Development of *Paulus*

Chronology

I strive to do my duty, and thus to win my Father's approval now as I
always formerly did, and devote to the completion of "St. Paul," in
which he took such pleasure, all the energies of my mind, to make it
as good as I possibly can."[1]

When Mendelssohn wrote *Paulus*, this oratorio seemed to him the most
important work of his young career. During the five years of work on
the oratorio, Mendelssohn started his professional career in Düsseldorf,
establishing himself as a conductor and a composer. While in Düsseldorf he explored different genres in church music, opera, and concert
music. After completing the first draft of *Paulus*, Mendelssohn moved
to Leipzig, finishing his first oratorio one year later. *Paulus* put on hold
Mendelssohn's lifelong search for an opera libretto, perhaps satisfying
temporarily his desire to compose a dramatic work. When Mendelssohn
began work on *Paulus*, he settled away from home for the first time.
Before he finished the oratorio his father died, and Mendelssohn had
found a new companion in Cécile Jeanrenaud. During the compositional phases of *Paulus*, Mendelssohn focused almost exclusively on
this one major work, limiting his other output to a few *Lieder* and piano

pieces. By the time Mendelssohn finished *Paulus*, it had become an immensely important part of his life.

Only half of the five years Mendelssohn worked on *Paulus* were spent on the music. He spent the first two and a half years on the libretto. The fact that Mendelssohn asked for help with the libretto from three different people—one musician, Adolf Bernhard Marx, and two theologians, Julius Fürst and Julius Schubring—shows the seriousness with which Mendelssohn approached his first oratorio; it also reflects the fact, however, that the composer was entering new territory.

The composition of *Paulus* falls into five phases. Each phase was equally intensive, and the oratorio was the main focus of Mendelssohn's work during those time periods. He set clear goals and deadlines for each of these phases. Although he reached or came very close to reaching his goals for these phases, it always took him more time than estimated. While Mendelssohn could have accomplished the composition of this quantity of music in less time, his high standards and his pursuit of the best product forced him to spend more time on each phase. Twice Mendelssohn canceled trips to England to continue working on *Paulus*. The deadline set by himself for finishing the oratorio was constantly moved back. Even taking the new position in Leipzig did not deter him from his conscientious work on the oratorio, despite his expressed desire to have *Paulus* finished while in Düsseldorf, "My obligations here end with the first of July; by then my oratorio, and I hope a new symphony and a piano concerto as well, will be finished, and the main purpose of my stay here, to be able to do my work in peace, will have been fulfilled."[2]

A look at the chronology of the autographs shows flexibility in approach and adaptability to the practical needs at hand. When Simrock wrote Mendelssohn that he wanted the piano-vocal score first, the composer, who had been working on a full score, started work on a piano-vocal score right away. A few months later, when Mendelssohn realized that he would not finish his revisions in time for the printing of a piano-vocal score of the complete oratorio before the premiere, he changed his plan and focused on revising the choruses first. These movements had to be finished first in order to have printed material for the large Festival choir, which was the only material that needed to be mass-produced for the first performance. During the revision process, Mendelssohn was always aware of what he needed to do because he was in close communication with the other parties involved.

Mendelssohn's Compositional
Approach to *Paulus*

First Draft

> When I am composing, I usually look at the Scriptural passages my-
> self, and thus you will find that much is simpler, shorter and more
> compressed than in your text; whereas at that time I could not get
> words enough, and was constantly longing for more. Since I have set
> to work, however, I feel very differently, and I can now make a selec-
> tion.[3]

During the composition of the initial draft, Mendelssohn worked from
several libretto drafts and the Bible. As he methodically composed the
oratorio from beginning to end, he changed the libretto frequently and
substantially. Although Mendelssohn started with the text, during the
process of composing the oratorio the text and the music influenced
each other, creating the single expression Mendelssohn wanted to convey.

Even though Mendelssohn worked on movements in order, he did
not number them during this first compositional phase. This might indicate that Mendelssohn saw the initial manuscript as a rough draft, but
it also shows that he was not thinking as much in terms of structure as
of content. In his first draft Mendelssohn expressed the story musically
as it unfolded in front of him in the libretto drafts and the Bible. Expression of content seemed more important at this stage than the structure of the oratorio.

Revision Phases

> There was much that pleased me at the performance, and much that
> dissatisfied me . . . so much is there that completely fails to express
> my idea—in fact does not even come near it. You have often advised
> me not to alter so much, and I am quite aware of the disadvantages of
> so doing; but if, on the other hand, I have been fortunate enough to
> render my idea in some parts of my work, and have no desire to
> change those, I cannot help but striving, on the other hand, to render
> my idea in other parts, and, if possible, throughout.[4]

It took Mendelssohn as long to revise *Paulus* as it did to compose the
first draft—twelve months. The autograph scores bear witness to the

complex, tedious, and tiresome process of revising. MN53 and MN54 show most of the layers of revision, from the initial draft to the performance. The fact that these autographs contain revised movements stemming from the initial version next to newly written or rewritten movements and every stage in between demonstrates Mendelssohn's careful and selective approach to revising. Mendelssohn did not revise *Paulus* out of insecurity; rather, he revised his work with confidence.

The longer the compositional process of his first oratorio continued, the clearer Mendelssohn's focus became about what he wanted to express and how to express it. Mendelssohn saw the compositional process of his first work in a new genre as a learning experience. He patiently and carefully examined his drafts and revised only what he thought did not convey his interpretation of the story of the apostle Paul.

During this process Mendelssohn asked and received criticism and help from friends and family. He valued the responses to content and presentation of his father, Abraham Mendelssohn, as much as the very specific criticism of his sister, Fanny Hensel. Comments of friends like Julius Schubring were welcome. Mendelssohn was not offended by, at times, strong criticism. All comments were evaluated and taken into account in the revision process.

Mendelssohn's Compositional Process

Initial Draft

> I have the second part now nearly all in my head, up to the passage where they take Paul for Jupiter, and wish to offer sacrifices to him, for which some fine choruses must be found, but as yet I have not the faintest conception what. . . . It is difficult.[5]

Mendelssohn wrote this in a letter to his mother a month before he started work on part 2 of the oratorio. There is no way of knowing whether and how extensively Mendelssohn had sketched any of these movements at that time. The only sketches that predate the first draft are found in MN19; it contains thematic sketches, short drafts, and a few continuity drafts. MN19 does not contain enough material of *Paulus* to make specific statements about Mendelssohn's working habits while working on the oratorio. All of the sketches and drafts show his normal habits of writing down important themes and writing down drafts of sections of movements in piano-score format.

It is impossible to say how often Mendelssohn routinely wrote down sketches and drafts for each movement first or if he composed some movements in full score. The amount of sketching for each movement must have depended on the complexity of the movement. The overture, with which Mendelssohn had a difficult time, was sketched out. In other instances Mendelssohn composed a movement in one day, which suggests that he had worked on this movement either in his head or on paper before writing it out in full score.[6]

The themes in MN19 are close to the themes that were eventually used; the longer drafts tend to be quite different from the later, complete versions. While it is unclear how much Mendelssohn routinely worked over a movement on paper before writing it out, it is obvious from the surviving movements of the first draft in MN53 and MN54 that Mendelssohn had formed clear ideas of the structure and content of each movement before committing it to paper in full score.

Revisions

The revisions were as complex as they were substantial. There is not a single movement that does not show revisions. Many movements were completely rewritten; other movements show eight layers of revisions. Even the rejected movements were revised before Mendelssohn cut them. A categorization of the different types of revisions help to gain a better understanding of the compositional process of *Paulus*.

Movement Plan

Table 3.3 (see page 31) shows ten rejected movements that were not replaced by movements with similar texts. One complete scene, Paul's imprisonment, was cut; another scene, Paul's missionary work to the Gentiles, was significantly shortened. Both of these substantial changes to the movement plan took place in part 2 of the oratorio. Mendelssohn was less sure of the content and movement structure of part 2 than he was of part 1. His lack of assurance regarding the content of part 2 of *Paulus* was mainly because the story line of part 1 was simpler. He did not have to select events for part 1 as carefully as for part 2. Consequently, the revisions to the movement plan of part 2 show a broader first draft, which was then narrowed down and focused in the subsequent drafts. These cuts of complete movements were therefore less musically motivated than they were interpretive choices about the content and the message of the oratorio. In cutting the three *Heidenchöre*, which Schubring suggested, as well as the cutting of Paul's imprisonment and miraculous release, Mendelssohn made a choice to focus less on the spectacular and more on the reflective, theological content, as well as on the character of Paul.

Other revisions to the movement plan of the oratorio were matters of timing within a scene. Mendelssohn was aware of the importance of the right dramatic speed of a scene, and on several occasions he changed the order of movements, cut movements, or changed the character of a movement and took control over the timing of a scene, maximizing its dramatic effect.

Choruses

The choruses show many structural, contrapuntal, harmonic, and voice-leading revisions. The main goal of all of Mendelssohn's revisions in the choruses was to gain clarity of expression.

Several choruses show substantial structural revision. Often these revisions were made to achieve a better proportional balance of the different sections of a movement. Such cuts were made in transitional sections; Mendelssohn would find more direct modulations, which would move more quickly to the next sections. Even in movements where Mendelssohn was not concerned about the proportions of the chorus, he often made cuts in transitional sections in order to tighten the structure of the movement.

Since the majority of his choruses show a polyphonic texture, many contrapuntal revisions are found in the choruses of *Paulus*. One important concern in Mendelssohn's contrapuntal revisions was the clear presentation and recurrence of the main thematic ideas throughout a chorus, because their appearance throughout a contrapuntal movement serve as guideposts to the listener. Often Mendelssohn revised the counterpoint around a subject to bring out the theme more strongly by changing the register or shortening the phrases of the other parts. The composer was also careful in his spacing of the appearances of themes. Sometimes he timed the spacing of entrances better; other times he moved the themes to different registers or vocal parts to gain control over the intensity level and overall structure by carefully spacing out the main entrances of themes in very high or very low registers. Regular entrance patterns of subjects were also important to Mendelssohn, and he would frequently revise imitative entrances so that they would follow clearer pitch patterns.

Text projection was another important element in Mendelssohn's contrapuntal revisions. Often he changed the syllable distribution and the rhythm of vocal parts in order to match the rhythm of the music to the rhythm of speech. The composer tended to create longer melismatic lines in the counterpoint to the main themes, which creates a better understanding of the text of the main theme. In other places Mendelssohn worked out the distribution of syllables better, creating better alignment in the texts of several vocal parts.

The smoothing out of vocal lines and the creating of better-defined, more expressive themes were concerns that are seen in the revisions of the polyphonic as well as the homophonic movements and passages. While Mendelssohn generally strove for smooth, simple vocal parts, he also chiseled out very carefully the shapes and characteristics of important themes. Rhythmic alterations played an important role in these revisions. The matching of the rhythm to the rhythm of the words was important, as was the use of rhythm to emphasize or de-emphasize certain phrases.

Along with the creation of better vocal lines, chord distribution was another aspect Mendelssohn took into consideration in his revisions of the vocal lines. From the first three chords of the opening chorus, where he redistributed the chord three times, throughout the whole oratorio, chord distribution along with syllabic changes were the most common and numerous revisions made in the choruses.

Recitatives

A few of the recitatives (in which the strength of the entire work resides) are really pointless or too modern.[7]

Nowhere were the revisions more drastic than in the recitatives. As Fanny Hensel remarks correctly, it is recitatives that make or break the oratorio, since they carry the action. Mendelssohn clearly was aware of the importance of the recitatives. Rather than having a piano-vocal score printed before the premiere, Mendelssohn took the time to revise the recitatives and arias once again.

Several times throughout the oratorio Mendelssohn changed the location of recitatives, contracting or dividing recitatives from earlier versions in his revisions. These revisions were made for structural reasons. Mendelssohn wanted to gain control over the dramatic flow of the oratorio by creating clear, self-contained scenes.

The revisions within most recitatives are numerous and often drastic. The goals of the revision of the vocal lines as well as the instrumental parts and the harmonic structure were to increase the expressiveness and to raise the intensity level of specific passages within each recitative. By doing so Mendelssohn created a more realistic, even theatrical, representation of the story. This is perhaps what Fanny Hensel described as "too modern." Even though Mendelssohn listened to most of his sister's criticisms, in this point Mendelssohn clearly had his own idea about the purpose and function of the recitatives in *Paulus*.

Another way in which Mendelssohn created a more realistic representation of the story was by his revisions regarding the distribution of vocal parts. While in the earlier version one soloist would sing a whole recitative regardless of the content, in his revisions throughout the oratorio Mendelssohn distributed parts spoken by specific characters to vocal parts other than the narrator in the recitative.

There are other examples where Mendelssohn changed his interpretation in his revisions. In the earlier versions Paul is portrayed as a strong, dogmatic, unbending man; in his revisions Mendelssohn understood Paul also as a gentle, loving person, which becomes the most obvious in Paul's reaction to his deification by the heathen (see chapter 5).

Arias

The arias show a combination of the revisions found in the recitatives and choruses. There are structural revisions for proportional purposes, as well as revisions to the vocal lines similar to those in the recitatives. The arias were the last group of movements Mendelssohn worked on immediately before the first performance. In fact, two arias were never inserted into MN54, because Mendelssohn did not finish revising them in time to be included in the autograph.

Instrumental Parts

The importance of Mendelssohn's revision of the orchestral score easily can be overlooked. Most of the time changes in the instrumental parts were made after the revision of the vocal parts, and often they are represented by separate layers in the scores. Mendelssohn made the orchestral score more transparent in his revisions by cutting doubled parts, thus thinning out the texture. Changes in the tone color of a section and the addition of articulations are other important revisions found in MN53 and MN54.

Mendelssohn's *Paulus* and the Oratorio in the Nineteenth Century

And I mainly want your opinion . . . if you think I could use chorales? I was most emphatically advised against it by Marx and others, and yet I cannot decide to give up the chorale completely, because I think that the chorale is a natural component of every oratorio from the New Testament.[8]

When Mendelssohn wrote this letter, six months before he started composing *Paulus*, he was still searching for the right format for his first oratorio. His leanings, however, already express his view of *Paulus* as music for edification rather than for entertainment. Partly because of the unpleasant ending of Mendelssohn's friendship with Marx, Mendelssohn relied throughout the compositional process more on Schubring's advice than anybody else's.[9] Ultimately, however, Mendelssohn made his own decisions about the form, structure, and content of his first oratorio. The decision on how to open the oratorio serves as a case in point. The use of a chorale (suggested by Schubring) within the context of a traditional French overture exemplifies Mendelssohn's synthesis of approaches found throughout the oratorio. While Mendelssohn intended for *Paulus* to espouse a Christian message, he nevertheless used all the tools of a dramatic stage work. With this approach Mendelssohn attempted to meet the challenge by his father to "solve the problem of combining ancient conceptions with modern appliances."[10]

The two main trends of the revision process confirm Mendelssohn's approach of combining the edifying elements of a Bach Passion with the style and musical expression of a nineteenth-century, highly dramatic style. One trend in all the revision stages of *Paulus* is not just the focus on the development of Paul's character before his conversion, during his conversion, and throughout his ministry until his eventual martyrdom for Christ, but even more the application of Paul's experience to the life of the Christian. Revisions such as establishing the chorale "Wachet auf!" as a theme for the oratorio, cutting more spectacular choruses and scenes in favor of sections reflective of Paul's faith, and changing the portrayal of Paul from that of an angry apostle to that of a gentle and loving missionary all show this trend.

The other main trend in Mendelssohn's revisions is the striving for a more realistic and intense representation of the story. The revisions of the recitatives clearly show this trend. The heightening of the expressiveness of the music, however, also can be seen in Mendelssohn's structural tightening of movements, in all the detailed contrapuntal, harmonic, and voice-leading revisions, and in the careful revisions to the instrumental parts.

Since Mendelssohn's second oratorio, *Elijah*, has been more popular in the twentieth century than the earlier *Paulus*, at least in the English-speaking countries, the danger exists of dismissing *Paulus* as merely a first attempt, from which Mendelssohn learned his lessons and eventually found the correct approach to the genre in his second oratorio. Rather than viewing *Elijah* as a progression from *Paulus*, these two oratorios should be regarded as complementary oratorios that display two different approaches because of their two different topics. *Paulus* is an oratorio based on a character of the New Testament; Paul is the most important teacher and writer in the history of Christianity. *Elijah*, however, is an oratorio based on the life of an Old Testament prophet. While Elijah's story can be viewed in a Christian context, the Christian applications of the story of Paul are much more immediate. Mendelssohn's comment to Schubring in connection with his question about the use of chorales indicates clearly that he made a distinction in his approach to stories of the Old Testament and the New Testament. To Mendelssohn an oratorio based on a New Testament story was— because of its more immediate relevance to Christian living—as much edificational as it was dramatic. An oratorio based on an Old Testament story, however, was to Mendelssohn more a historical topic and did not call for the reflective, congregational responses to the content of the oratorio. Possibly Mendelssohn's dual background in Judaism and Christianity created this clear distinction between the Old Testament and the New Testament. The best evidence for Mendelssohn's dual approach to the oratoric genre can be found in the fragments of Mendelssohn's third oratorio, *Christus*. The use of chorales in these fragments shows Mendelssohn's approach as similar to his approach to *Paulus*; it validates the composer's first oratorio not just as a first step in a new genre, but as a defined, well-thought-out approach.

Notes

1. Felix Mendelssohn, *Letters from 1833 to 1847*, to Pastor Bauer, 9 December 1835, 90.

2. Felix Mendelssohn, *A Life in Letters*, 15 January 1835, 205.

3. Felix Mendelssohn, *Letters from 1833 to 1847*, 20 July 1835, 39-40.

4. Felix Mendelssohn, *Letters of Felix Mendelssohn to Ignaz and Charlotte Moscheles*, 20 July 1836, 149.

5. Felix Mendelssohn, *Letters from 1833 to 1847*, to Lea Mendelssohn, 4 November 1834, 50.

6. Felix Mendelssohn, *Letters of Felix Mendelssohn to Ignaz and Charlotte Moscheles*, 7 February 1835, 126: "To-day I composed a chorus for my Oratorio, and I am quite pleased with it."

7. Fanny Hensel, *The Letters of Fanny Hensel to Felix Mendelssohn*, 4 February 1836, 199.

8. Felix Mendelssohn, *Briefwechsel zwischen Felix Mendelssohn und J. Schubring zugleich ein Beitrag zur Geschichte des Oratoriums*, 6 September 1833, 41: Dann aber wünsche ich hauptsächlich deine Meinung . . . ob du meinst, ich könne den Choral drin haben? Mir ist von Marx und andern sehr entschieden abgeredet worden, und doch kann ich mich nicht entschließen ihn ganz aufzugeben, denn ich denke, in jedem Oratorium aus dem neuen Testament müsse er von Natur sein.

9. Eric Werner, *Mendelssohn: A New Image of the Composer and His Age* (New York: Free Press of Glencoe, 1963), 280-81.

10. Abraham Mendelssohn, *Letters from 1833 to 1847*, 10 March 1835, 72.

Appendix A

The Structure and Content of MN53

(The dotted horizontal lines mark the foliation of the manuscript; the "T" after a paper type letter denotes leafs or bifolios that were used turned around)

Page numberings			Contents	Paper type
1			title page	
[2]				
3		1	first page of music; "Overtüre"; "Hilf Du mir"	A
[4]		2		A
5	2	3		A
[6]		4		A
7	3	5		AT
[8]		6		AT
9	4	7		AT
[10]		8		AT
11	5	9		AT
[12]		10		AT
13	6	11		B
[14]		12		B
15	7	13		B
[16]		14		B
17	8	15		B
[18]		16		B
19	9	17		B
[20]		18		B
21	10	19	1 No. 2 Chor "Herr, der du bist der Gott"	C
[22]		20	2	C
23	11	21	3	C
[24]		22	4	C
25	12	23	5	C
[26]		24	6	C
27	13	25	7	C
[28]		26	8	C
29	14	27	9	C
[30]		28	10	C
31	15	29		C
[32]		30		C
33	16	31		C

Continued on next page

213

Page numberings					Contents	Paper type
[34]		32				C
35	17	33				CT
[36]		34				CT
37	18	35				CT
[38]		36				CT
39	19	37		19		C
[40]		38		20		C
41	20	39		21		C
[42]		40		22		C
43	21	41		22	No. 3 Recit. "Die Menge der Gläubigen"	C
[44]		42				C
45	22	44	43a	23	No. 4 [2] Choral "Allein Gott in der Höh"	C
[46]		45		24	No. 5 Recit. "Stephanus aber voll Glaubens"	C
47	23	46			No. 4 Recit. "Die Menge der Gläubigen"; upper two thirds crossed out	C
[48]		47			most of page crossed out; [Duet] "Wir haben ihn gehört"	C
49	24	48				C
[50]		49			[Recit.] "Und bewegten das Volk"	C
51	25	50			paste-over	CT
[52]		51		4	No. 6 [4; 5 (pencil)] Coro "Dieser Mensch hört nicht auf"	CT
53	26	52		5		CT
[54]		53		6		CT
55	27	54		7		CT
[56]		55		8		CT
57	28	56		9		CT
[58]		57		10		CT
59	29	58				C
[60]		59				C
61	30	60				C
[62]		61				C
63	31	62		15		CT
[64]		63		16		CT
65	32	64		17		CT
[66]		65		18		CT
67	33	66		19		CT
[68]		67		20		CT
69	34	68		21	No. 7 [5 (pencil); 7] Recitativo "Und sie sahen auf ihn alle"	A
[70]		69		22	paste-over over lower system, taken out	A
71	35	70				AT
[72]		71			[Recit.] "Ihr Halsstarrigen"	AT
73	36	72				AT
[74]		73			[Chor] "Weg weg mit dem"	AT
75	37	74		??	[Recit.] "Siehe, ich sehe den Himmel offen"	B
[76]		75			No. 8 Aria [6 (pencil); 8] "Jerusalem"	B

Continued on next page

Page numberings					Contents	Paper type
77	38	76				B
[78]		77				B
79	39	78				B
[80]		79			No. 9 [7, 8] Recit. "Sie aber stürmten auf ihn ein"; Chor "Steiniget ihn"	B
81	40	80			copyist's number, "1"	B
[82]		81			copyist's numbers, "2" and "3"	B
83	41	82			copyist's number, "4"	B
[84]		83			copyist's numbers, "5" and "6"	B
85	42	84			copyist's number, "7"	B
[86]		85			copyist's numbers, "8" and "9"	B
87	43	86	1		No. 10 Recitativo "Und sie steinigten ihn"	CT
[88]			2		Choral "Dir Herr will ich mich ergeben"	CT
89	44	88	3			CT
[90]			4		No. 11 Arie "Der du die Menschen läßest sterben"; written above "[illegible word] nach No. 9"	CT
91	45	90	5		"x" in soprano in red pencil	B
[92]			6			B
93	46	92	7			B
[94]			8		No. 12 Recit. "Es bestellten aber Stephanum"; "x" at bottom of page in red pencil	B
95	47	94	9	41	No. 13 Chor [9] "Siehe wir preisen selig"	A
[96]				42		A
97	48			43		A
[98]			10	44	"x" at top of page in black ink	A
99	49		11	45		A
[100]			12	46		A
101	50		13	47		A
[102]			14	48		A
103	51		15	49		A
[104]			16	50		A
105	52		17	51		A
[106]			18	52		A
107	53		19			AT
[108]			20		No. 14 Recit. "Und die Zeugen hatten abgelegt ihre Kleider"; [Arie] "Vertilge sie"	AT
109	54		21			AT
[110]			22			AT
111	55		23			B
[112]			24			B
113	56		25			B
[114]			26			B
115	57		27		No. 15 Recit. "Und Paulus zerstörte die Gemeinde"	B
[116]			28		No. 16 Arioso "Doch der Herr vergißt der Seinen nicht"	B
117	58		29		No. 17 Recit. mit Chor "Und als er auf dem Wege war"; "Saul was verfolgtst du mich"	B

Continued on next page

Page numberings			Contents	Paper type
[118]		30		B
119	59	31		B
[120]		32		B
121	60	33		CT
[122]		34		CT
123	61	35	No. 18 [15] Chor "Mache dich auf werde Licht"	CT
[124]		36		CT
125	62	37		A
[126]		38		A
127	63	39		A
[128]		40		A
129	64	41		A
[130]		42		A
131	65	43		A
[132]		44		A
133	66	45		A
[134]		46		A
135	67	47		A
[136]		48		A
137	68	49		A
[138]		50		A
139	69	51		A
[140]		52		A
141	70	53		A
[142]		54		A
143	71	55		A
[144]		56	No. 19 [16] Choral "Wachet auf ruft uns die Stimme"	A
145	72	57		A
[146]		58		A
147	73	59		A
[148]		60		A
149	74	61	No. 20 [17] Recit. "Die Männer aber, die seine Gefährten waren"	C
[150]		62		C
151	75	63	No. 21 [18] Aria "Gott sei mir gnädig"	C
[152]		64		C
153	76	65		C
[154]		66		C
155	77	67		B
[156]		68		B
157	78	69		C
[158]		70		C
159	79	71	No. 22 [19] Recitativo "Es war aber ein Jüngling zu Damascus"	C
[160]		72		C
161	80	73	No. 23 [20] Aria und Chor "Ich danke dir Herr mein Gott"; "Der Herr wird die Tränen"	C

Continued on next page

Page numberings			Contents	Paper type
[162]		74		C
163	81	75		C
[164]		76		C
165	82	77		C
[166]		78		C
167	83	79		CT
[168]		80		CT
169	84	81		CT
172		82	vertical paste-over—half-page	CT
173	85	83	whole page crossed out	CT
[174]		84		CT
175	86	85		CT
[176]		86		CT
177	87	87		C
[178]		88		C
179	88	89		C
[180]		90	No. 24 [21] Recitativo "Und Ananias ging hin"	C
181	89	91		C
[182]		92		C
183	90	93		C
[184]		94		C
185	91	95		C
[186]		96		C
187	92	97	No. 25 [22] Chor "O welch eine Tiefe"	A
[188]		98		A
189	93	99		A
[190]		100		A
191	94	101		A
[192]		*102		A
193	95	103		A
[194]		104		A
195	96	105		A
198		106	paste-over over music, other side is empty	A
199	97	107		A
[200]		108		A
201	98	109		A
204		110	paste-over	AT
205	99	111	whole page crossed out	A
[206]		112		A
207	100	113		A
[208]		114		A
209	101	115		A
[210]		116		A
211	102	117	"Ende des ersten Theils" (black ink)—"Leipzig den 8ten April 1836" (brown ink)—crossed-out material on back, back pasted to binding page	A

Appendix B

The Structure and Content of MN54

Page numberings			Contents	Paper type
[1]	1		"Paulus, Zweiter Theil," No. 26 Chor "Der Erdkreis ist nun des Herrn"	B
[2]	2			B
[3]	3			B
[4]	4			B
[5]	5			B
[6]	6			B
[7]	7		copyist's number, "6"	B
[8]	8			B
[9]	9			A
[10]	10			A
[11]	11			A
[12]	12			A
[13]	13			B
[14]	14		No. 27 Recit. "Und Paulus kam zu der Gemeinde"	B
[15]	15		No. 28 Duettino "So sind wir nun Botschafter"	C
[16]	16			C
[17]	17			C
[18]	18			C
[19]	19	10		C
[20]	20		No. 29 Chor "Wie lieblich sind die Boten"	C
[21]	21			C
[22]	22			C
[23]	23			C
[24]	24			C
[25]	25			C
[26]	26			C
[27]	27			C
[28]	28			C
[29]	29			C
[30]	30			C
31	30a		No. 30 Arioso "Laßt uns singen von der Gnade"	CT
[32]	30b			CT
33	30c			CT
[34]	30c			CT

Continued on next page

Page numberings			Contents	Paper type
35	31		last 2 mm. of No. 29; No. 30 Rec. "Und wie sie ausge-sandt"; "folgt eine Arie"; "Da aber die Juden das Volk sahen"	C
[36]	32		Chor "So spricht der Herr"	C
37	33			C
[38]	34			C
39	35	20	No. 31 Recit. "Und sie stellten Paulus nach"	C
[40]	36		Chor "Ist das nicht"	C
41	37			C
[42]	38			C
43	39			C
[44]	40			C
45	41			C
[46]	42			C
47	43		watermark "C.F." at bottom of bifolio	C
[48]	44		[Choral] "O Jesu Christe"	C
49	45			C
[50]	46			C
51	47			C
[52]	48			C
53	49			C
[54]	50			C
55	1		No. 32 Recit. "Da sprach Paulus zu ihnen"; "hier folgt eine Arie"(pencil); No. 33 Recit. "Da das aber die Heiden hörten"	B
[56]				B
57			Chor "Die Götter sind den Menschen"	B
[58]				B
59	2	30		B
[60]				B
61				B
[62]				B
63	3		No. 34 Recit. "Und nannten Barnabas Jupiter"	C
[64]			No. 35 Chor "Seyd uns gnädig hohe Götter"	C
65				C
[66]				C
67	4			C
[68]				C
69				C
[70]				C
71	5			C
[72]			No. 36 Recitativo "Da das die Apostel hörten"	C
73				C
[74]				C
75	[6]		[No. 37 Arie] "Wisset ihr nicht"	CT
[76]				CT
77				CT

Continued on next page

Page numberings			Contents	Paper type
[78]				CT
79	7	40	No. 38 Chor "Aber unser Gott"; "38" written again because of ink spill	A
[80]				A
81				A
[82]				A
83	[8]			A
[84]				A
85				A
[86]			No. 39 Recit. "Da ward das Volk erreget"; No.40 Chor "Hier ist des Herren Tempel"	A
87	9			B
[88]				B
89				B
[90]				B
91	10			B
[92]				B
93				B
[94]			No. 41 Recit. "Und sie alle verfolgten Paulus"	B
95	11		Cavatina "Sey getreu bis in den Tod"	A
[96]				A
97				A
[98]				A
99	12	50	No. 42 Choral "Erhebe dich o meine Seel"	B
[100]			No. 43 Rec. u. Chor "Paulus sandte hin"	B
101			[Chor] "Schone doch deiner selbst"	B
[102]				B
103	13		copyist's number, "4"	C
[104]			copyist's number, "6"	C
105			[Recit.] "Was machet ihr"	C
[106]				C
107	14		[Chor] "Des Herrn Wille geschehe"	C
[108]			[Recit.] "Und als er das gesagt"	C
109				C
[110]			No. 44 Chor "Sehet, welch eine Liebe"	C
111	15			C
[112]			copyist's number, "1"	C
113			copyist's number, "2"	C
[114]			copyist's number, "3"	C
115	16		copyist's number, "4"	C
[116]			copyist's number, "5"	C
117				C
[118]			No. 45 Recit "Und wenn er schon geopfert wird"	C
119	17	60		A
[120]			No. 46 Schluß=Chor "Nicht aber ihm sondern allen"	A
121				A

Continued on next page

Page numberings			Contents	Paper type
[122]				A
12?	18			A
[124]				A
125				A
[126]				A
127	19			A
[128]				A
129				A
[130]				A
131	20			A
[132]				A
133			copyist's number, "1"	A
[134]			copyist's number, "2"	A
135	21		copyist's number ,"4"	A
[136]			copyist's number, "6"	A
137		68	copyist's number, "8"	A
[138]			"Leipzig den 18ten April 1836"	A

Appendix C

The Structure and Content of MN55

Page numberings		Contents	Paper type
		title page	B
		"No. 1 Ouverture"—"Secondo"—page crossed out in pencil	B
2		"No. 1 Ouverture"—"Primo"—page crossed out in pencil	B
		"Secondo"	B
3		"Primo"	B
		"Secondo"	B
4		"Primo"	B
		"Primo"—"Secondo"	B
5	1	"Auf die Ouverture"; No. 2 Chor "Herr, der du bist der Gott"	C
			C
6			C
			C
7	2		C
			C
8		"x"-markings in piano part in pencil	C
			C
9	3		C
		No. 3 Recit "Die Menge der Gläubigen," "Choral" crossed out; No. 4 Choral "Allein Gott in der Höh sei Ehr"	C
10		No. 5 Recit. "Stephanus aber voll Glaubens"	C
		[Duet] "Wir haben ihn gehört"	C
11	4	Rec. "Da bewegten sie das Volk"	C
		No. 6 Chor "Dieser Mensch hört nicht auf"	C
12			C
		"x"-marking lower system in pencil	C
13	5		C
			C
14			C
			C
15	6	No. 7 Recit. "Und sie sahen auf ihn alle"	B
			B
16			B
		[Chor] "Weg weg mit ihm"	B
17	7		B
		No. 8 Arioso "Jerusalem"; "x" marks in pencil	B

Continued on next page

223

Page numberings		Contents	Paper type
18		No. 9 Recit. "Sie aber stürmten auf ihn ein"; Chor "Steiniget ihn"; "x" marks in pencil	B
			B
19	8		C
			C
20			C
		empty page	C
21	9	No. 10 Recit. "Und sie steinigten ihn"; Choral "Dir Herr will ich mich ergeben"	B
		No. 11 Arioso "Der du die Menschen lässest sterben"	B
22			B
		No. 12 Recit. "Es bestellten aber"; No.13 Chor "Siehe, wie preisen selig"	B
23	10	"head" sign in pencil	C
			C
24		"head" sign in pencil	C
			C
25	11	"head" sign in pencil	C
			C
26		No. 14 Recit. "Und die Zeugen hatten abgelegt"; bottom system crossed out in pencil ("Vertilge sie")	C
		whole page crossed out in pencil	C
27	12	whole page crossed out in pencil	B
		whole page crossed out in pencil	B
28		whole page crossed out in pencil	B
		No. 15 Recit. "Und Paulus zerstörte"; "hier folgt eine Arie" written underneath recit.	B
29	1	No.17 Recit. "Und als er auf dem Wege war"; "4" changed to "7"	B
		No. 18 Chor "Mache dich auf"; "5" changed to "8"	B
30			B
		"head" sign in pencil	B
31	2	"head" sign in pencil	C
		"x" mark in pencil; copyist's number, "14"	C
32		copyist's numbers, "15" and "16"; "head" sign in pencil	C
		"x" written in pencil; copyist's numbers, "17" and "18"	C
33	3	copyist's number, "19"	C
		copyist's numbers, "20" and "21"; "head" sign in pencil	C
34			C
		copyist's numbers, "23" and "24"; "x" and "head" sign in pencil	C
35	4	copyist's number, "25"	C
		No. 19 Choral "Wachet auf ruft uns die Stimme"; "6" changed to "9"; "head" sign in pencil; "27" written in black ink	C
36			C
		copyist's number, "29" and "30"	C
37	5	No. 20 [17] Recit. "Die Männer aber"; copyist's number, "31"	C
		No. 21 [18] Aria "Gott sei mir gnädig"; copyist's number, "32"	C
38		copyist's number, "33"	C

Continued on next page

Page numberings		Contents	Paper type
		copyist's numbers, "34" and "35"	C
39	6	copyist's number, "36"	C
		No. 22 [19] Recit. "Es war aber ein Jüngling"; copyist's numbers, "37" and "38"	C
40		No. 23 [20] Arie mit Chor "Ich danke dir Herr mein Gott"; copyist's number, "39"	C
		copyist's number, "40"	C
41	7	[Chor] "Der Herr wird die Tränen"; copyist's number, "41" and "42"; "head" sign written in pencil	C
		copyist's numbers, "43" and "44"	C
42		"x" and "head" sign in pencil; copyist's number, "45"	C
		copyist's numbers, "46" and "47"	C
43	8	copyist's numbers, "48" (black ink), "49" (pencil)	C
		copyist's number, "50" (pencil); "x" and head sign in pencil	C
44		copyist's numbers, "51," "52" (pencil); No. 24 [21] Recit. "Und Ananias ging hin"; "x" in pencil	C
		copyist's numbers, "53" and "54"	C
45	9	No. 25 [22] Chor "O welch eine Tiefe"; copyist's number, "55"	C
		copyist's numbers, "56" and "57"	C
46		copyist's numbers, "58" and "59"; "x" in pencil	C
		copyist's numbers, "60" and "61"; "x" in pencil	C
47	10	copyist's numbers, "62" and "63"; "x" and "head" sign in pencil	C
		copyist's number, "64" (pencil)	C
48		copyist's numbers, "65" and "66"; lighter corr. in pencil	C
		copyist's numbers, "67" and "68"; "x" in pencil	C
49	11	copyist's numbers, "70" and "70" (pencil)	C
		copyist's number, "71" (pencil)	C
50		copyist's number, "72" (pencil)	C
		copyist's numbers, "74" and "75"; also "58" (pencil)	C
51		copyist's number, "76"; "Ende des ersten Theils"	C
		"Zweiter Theil"; Chor "Die Nacht ist vergangen"; whole page crossed out in red pencil	C
52		empty page	B
		No. 26 Chor "Der Erdkreis ist nun des Herrn"	B
53	1	No. 26 Chor "Der Erdkreis ist nun des Herrn"; measures of previous page crossed out	B
	2		B
54	3		B
	4		B
55	5		B
	6		B
56	7		B
	8		B
57	9	copyist's number, "68"	B
		empty page	B
58	11	No. 27 Recit. "Und Paulus kam zu der Gemeinde"; No. 28 Duettino "So sind wir nun Botschafter"	C

Continued on next page

Page numberings			Contents	Paper type
				C
59	13		No. 29 [30] Chor "Wie lieblich sind die Boten"	C
				C
60	15			C
			"x" in black ink	C
61	17		paste-over; "x" in pencil	C
				C
62			No. 30 Arioso "Laßt uns singen von der Gnade"; "nach no. 30 mit Freudigkeit" written at the top	C
				C
63	19		No. 30 Recit. "Und wie sie ausgesandt"; "Da aber die Juden das Volk sahen"	B
			No. 31 Chor "So spricht der Herr"; "No. 31" crossed out	B
64	20	21	No. 31 Recit. "Und sie stellten Paulus nach"; "No. 31" in pencil; Chor "Ist das nicht"	B
				B
65	21			C
				C
66	22			C
				C
67	23		[Choral] "O Jesu Christe"	C
				C
68	24			C
				C
69	25		No. 32 [33] Recit. "Paulus aber und Barnabas"	B
			Chor "Die Götter sind den Menschen"	B
70	26			B
				B
71	27		No. 34 Recit. "Und nannten Barnabas Jupiter," "5" changed to "4" (pencil)	C
			No. 35 [36] Chor "Seid uns gnädig"	C
72	28			C
				C
73	29			C
			No. 36 Recit. "Da das die Apostel hörten" crossed out (pencil); "36" written in pencil	C
74	30		[No. 37 Aria ending with:] ". . . Aber unser Gott ist im Himmel"; No. 38 Chor "Aber unser Gott"; "No. 38" in pencil	C
				C
75	31			C
				C
76	32			C
				C
77	33		No. 39 Arioso "Wisset ihr nicht"; "No. 39" written in pencil, music for "Arioso" crossed out (pencil)	C

Continued on next page

Page numberings			Contents	Paper type
			continued Arioso crossed out, Recit. "Da ward das Volk erreget"	C
78	34		No.40 Chor "Hier ist des Herren Tempel"; "No 40" in pencil	C
				C
79	35			C
				C
80	36			C
			No. 41 Recit. "Und alles Volk verfolgte"; "No. 41" in pencil	C
81		1	"H. d. m." ["Hilf du mir"] at top of the page; [Cavatina] "Sey getreu bis in den Tod"	C
				C
82		2		C
			empty page	C
83	37		"hier folgt eine Cavatina" written in pencil; No. 42 Choral "Erhebe dich o meine Seel"; "No. 42" written in pencil	C
				C
84	38		No. 43 Recit. "Paulus sandte hin," "No. 43" in pencil; Chor "Schone doch deiner selbst"	B
				B
85	39			B
			Recit. "Was macht ihr da"	B
86	40	1	Chor "Des Herrn Wille geschehe"; Recit. "Und als er das gesagt"	B
		2	No.44 Chor "Sehet welch eine Liebe"; "No. 44" in pencil	B
87	41	3		B
				B
88	42			C
			No. 45 Recit. "Und wenn er schon geopfert wird"; "No. 45" in pencil	C
89	43	1	No. 46 Schluß=Chor "Nicht aber ihm allein"; "No. 46" in pencil	C
				C
90	44	2		C
				C
91	45	3		C
				C
92	46			C
				C
93	47	5		C
				C
94	48	6		C
			last page of music	C

Appendix D

The Structure and Content of MN28

Page numbers	Contents	Paper type
169	No. 2 Choral "Ach bleibe mit deiner Gnade"	C
[170]		C
171		C
[172]		C
173	end of movement	C
[174]	No. 3 Recit. "Die Menge der Gläubigen war ein Herz," incomplete	C
[175]	No. 13 Chor "Herr Gott, de die Rache ist erscheine"	CT
[176]		CT
177		C
[178]		C
179		C
[180]		C
181		C
[182]	copyist's number, "8"	C
183		C
[184]		C
185		C
[186]		C
187		C
[188]		C
189	one measure of a previous movement; Chorus "Lobt ihn mit Pfeifen"	A
[190]		A
191		AT
[192]		AT
193		AT
[194]		AT
195		AT
[196]		AT
197		AT
[198]		AT
199		A
[200]		A
201		A
[202]		A
203		A
[204]		A

Continued on next page

Page numbers	Contents	Paper type
205		A
[206]		A
207		AT
[208]		AT
209		AT
[210]		AT
211		AT
[212]		AT
213		AT
[214]		AT
215		AT
[216]	end of movement	AT
217	Chorus "Danket dem Gott"; "Danket dem Herrn"	A
[218]		A
219		A
[220]		A
221	end of movement	AT
[222]	empty page	AT
223	No. 32 Chor "Danket den Gttern"	AT
[224]		AT
225		AT
[226]		AT
227		A
[228]		A
229		A
[230]		A
231		A
[232]		A
233		A
[234]	empty page	A
235	[Duet] "Gelobet sei Gott der Vater unseres Herrn"	AT
[236]		AT
237		AT
[238]		AT
239		AT
[240]		AT
241		AT
[242]		AT
243	end of movement	AT
[244]	Recit. "Schnell aber ward ein groes Erdbeben"	AT
245		AT
[246]		AT
247	end of movement; Choral "O treuer Heiland Jesu Christ"	AT
[248]	end of Chorale; Recit. "Paulus sandte hin"	AT
249		AT
[250]	end of recitative; Chor "Schone doch deiner selbst"	AT
251	No. 28 Recit. "Die unter Euch Gott frchten"	CT

Continued on next page

Page numbers	Contents	Paper type
[252]		CT
253		A
[254]	Recitative leads into [Choral] "Mit unser Macht" [A mighty fortress]	A
255		A
[256]		A
257		AT
[258]		AT
259		AT
[260]		AT

Bibliography

Sources of *Paulus*

Bibliotheque du Conservatoire Royal de Musique Brussels (B-BC)

Ms. 1092—leaf of an earlier version of "Steiniget ihn" (No. 9).

Staatsbibliothek zu Berlin—Preußischer Kulturbesitz (D-B)

Mus. ms. autogr. Mendelssohn [MN] 19—sketches.
Mus. ms. autogr. Mendelssohn [MN] 28—discarded movements.
Mus. ms. autogr. Mendelssohn [MN] 20—pp. 55-57, handcopy of "Doch der Herr," op. 112, by Marie Mendelssohn.

Hessische Landes- und Hochschulbibliothek Darmstadt (D-DS)

Mus. ms. 1445b—first page of one leaf containing "Doch Der Herr er leitet die Irrenden recht," op. 112 Nr. 1, originally intended for *Paulus*.

Biblioteka Jagiellonska Kraków (P-Kj)

Mus. ms. autogr. Mendelssohn [MN] 53—part I of manuscript score of *Paulus*.
Mus. ms. autogr. Mendelssohn [MN] 54—part II of manuscript score of *Paulus*.
Mus. ms. autogr. Mendelssohn [MN] 55—piano-vocal score of *Paulus*.

New York Public Library New York (US-NYp)

Drexel Collection 4779—manuscript copy of piano-vocal score used in preparation of Düsseldorf performance.

Stanford University Library Stanford, California (US-STu)

One page of musical memento written by Mendelssohn containing the opening theme of "So sind wir denn nun Botschafter."

Simrock Archives, Anton Benjamin, Hamburg

Korrekturabzug (plate number 3320) of *Paulus*

Editions of *Paulus*

Bonn: Simrock; London: Novello, 1836—piano-vocal score.
London: Novello, 1836—piano-vocal score in English.
Bonn: Simrock; London: Novello, 1837—full score.
Felix Mendelssohn's Werke. Kritisch durchgesehene Ausgabe: Serie 13/1. Edited by Julius Rietz. Leipzig: Breitkopf und Härtel, 1847-77.
Critical edition by Larry Todd. Stuttgart: Carus, 1997.

Published Letters

Devrient, Eduard. *Meine Erinnerungen an Felix Mendelssohn-Bartholdy und seine Briefe an mich*. Leipzig: Weber, 1869.
Hensel, Fanny. *The Letters of Fanny Hensel to Felix Mendelssohn*. Ed. and trans. by Marcia J. Citron. New York: Pendragon Press, 1987.
Hensel, Sebastian. *Die Familie Mendelssohn, 1729-1847. Nach Briefen und Tagebüchern*. Berlin: Behr, 1891. Published in English under the title *The Mendelssohn Family (1729-1847) from Letters and Journals*. Translated by Carl Klingemann. New York: Harper, 1881.
Hiller, Ferdinand. *Felix Mendelssohn: Briefe und Erinnerungen*. Cologne: Dumont Schauburg, 1874. Published in English under the title *Mendelssohn. Letters and Recollections*. Translated by M.E. von Glehn. London: Macmillan, 1874.
Klingemann, Karl, ed. *Felix Mendelssohn-Bartholdy. Briefe und Erinnerungen*. Essen: Baedeker, 1909.
Mendelssohn, Felix. *Letters of Felix Mendelssohn to Ignaz and Charlotte Moscheles*. Ed. and trans. by Felix Moscheles. Boston: Ticknor, 1888.

————. *Briefe an deutsche Verleger*. Ed. Rudolf Elvers. Berlin: Walter de Gruyter & Co., 1968.

————. *Felix Mendelssohn Bartholdy: Briefe*. Ed. Rudolf Elvers. Franfurt: Fischer, 1984.

————. *Briefe aus Leipziger Archiven*. Ed. Hans-Joachim Rothe, Reinhard Szeskus. Leipzig: Deutscher Verlag für Musik, 1972.

————. *Felix Mendelssohn-Bartholdys Briefwechsel mit Legationsrat Karl Klingemann in London*. Ed. Karl Klingemann Jr. Essen: G.D. Baedeker, 1909.

————. *Letters*. Ed. G. Selden-Goth. New York: Pantheon, 1945.

————. *Letters from 1833 to 1847*. Ed. Paul and Carl Mendelssohn-Bartholdy. Translated by Lady Wallace. London: Longman, Green and Co., 1890.

————. *Letters from Italy and Switzerland*. Translated by Lady Wallace. London: Longman, Green and Co., 1862.

————. *A Life in Letters*. Ed. Rudolf Elvers. Translated by Craig Tomlinson. New York: Fromm, 1986

Schubring, Julius, ed. *Briefwechsel zwischen Felix Mendelssohn und J. Schubring; zugleich ein Beitrag zur Geschichte des Oratoriums*. Leipzig: Duncker & Humblot, 1892.

Unpublished letters

Collection Deneke, Bodleian Library, Oxford.
Landesbibliothek Düsseldorf.
Heinrich-Heine-Institut Düsseldorf, Musikvereinsdeposit.
New York Public Library.

Paulus

Chorley, Henry. [About *Paulus*]. *Athenaeum* 11 (1837): 709.

Dahlhaus, Carl. "Mendelssohn und die musikalische Gattungstradition." In *Das Problem Mendelssohn*, 55-60. Regensburg: Bosse, 1974.

Edwards, Frederick George. "Mendelssohn's St. Paul." *The Musical Times* 32 (1891): 137-38.

Fink, Gottfried Wilhelm. "Paulus." *Allgemeine musikalische Zeitung* 39/31-32 (1837): cols. 497-506, 513-30.

Giehne, Heinrich. *Paulus*. Karlsruhe, 1846.

Grove, George. "Mendelssohn's oratorio 'St. Paul.'" *The Musical Times* 49 (1909): 92-94.

Jahn, Otto. *Über Felix Mendelssohn Bartholdy's Oratorium Paulus.* Kiel: 1842. Also in *Allgemeine musikalische Zeitung* 50 (1848): cols. 113-22, 137-43, and in *Gesammelte Aufsätze über Musik.* Leipzig: Breitkopf und Härtel, 1866.

Keferstein, G.A.. "Das Oratorium." *Allgemeine musikalische Zeitung* 50/49-51 (1843): cols. 873-79, 897-902, 921-26.

Krummacher, Friedhelm. "Religiosität und Kunstcharacter: über Mendelssohns Oratorium Paulus." In *Geistliche Musik: Studien zu ihrer Geschichte und Funktion im 18. und 19. Jahrhundert*, edited by C. Floros, Hamburger Jahrbuch für Musikwissenschaft, vol. 8, 97-117. Laaber: Laaber, 1985.

Kurzhals-Reuter, Arntrud. *Die Oratorien Felix Mendelssohn Bartholdys:Untersuchungen zur Quellenlage, Entstehung, Gestaltung und Überlieferung.* Tutzing: Hans Schneider, 1978.

Meiser, Martin. "Das Paulusbild bei Mendelssohn und Mendelssohns christliche Selbsterfahrung." *Musik und Kirche* 62/5 (Sep./Oct. 1992): 259-64.

Mosewius, Johann Theodor. *Zur Aufführung des Oratoriums "Paulus."* Breslau: n.p. 1837.

Reimer, Erich. "Mendelssohns 'edler Gesang': Zur Kompositionsweise der Sologesänge im *Paulus*." *Archiv für Musikwissenschaft* 50/1 (1993): 44-70.

————. "Textanlage und Szenengestaltung in Mendelssohns *Paulus*." *Archiv für Musikwissenschaft* 46/1 (1989): 42-69.

Mendelssohn's Sacred Music

Brodbeck, David. "A Winter of Discontent: Mendelssohn and the *Berliner Domchor*." In *Mendelssohn Studies*, edited by R. Larry Todd, 1-32. Cambridge: Cambridge University Press, 1992.

Clostermann, Annemarie. *Mendelssohn Bartholdys kirchenmusikalisches Schaffen: Neue Untersuchungen zu Geschichte, Form und Inhalt.* Mainz: Schott, 1989.

Dinglinger, Wolfgang. *Studien zu den Psalmen mit Orchester von Felix Mendelssohn Bartholdy.* Köln: Studio, 1993.

Feder, Georg. "Verfall und Restauration." In *Geschichte der Evangelischen Kirchenmusik*, edited by Friedrich Blume, 215-70. Kassel: Bärenreiter, 1965.

————. "Zwischen Kirche und Konzertsaal: Zu Felix Mendelssohn Bartholdys geistlicher Musik." In *Religiöse Musik in nichtliturgischen Werken von Beethoven bis Reger*, 97-118. Regensburg: Bosse, 1978.

Grossmann-Vendrey, Susanna. *Felix Mendelssohn Bartholdy und die Musik der Vergangenheit*. Regensburg: Bosse, 1969.

Hiromi, Hoshino. "Die geistliche Vokalmusik Felix Mendelssohn Bartholdys: Untersuchungen zu ihrer stilistischen Entwicklung." *Journal of the Musicological Society of Japan* 41/1 (1995): 33-56.

Sposato, Jeffrey. *Mendelssohn's Theological Evolution: A Study of Texual Choice and Change in the Composer's Sacred Works*. Ph.D. diss., Brandeis University, forthcoming.

Werner, Rudolf. *Felix Mendelssohn Bartholdy als Kirchenmusiker*. Frankfurt: Rudolf Werner, 1930.

Mendelssohn's Compositional Process

Gerlach, Reinhard. "Mendelssohns Kompositionsweise. Vergleich zwischen Skizzen und Letztfassung des Violinkonzertes opus 64." *Archiv für Musikwissenschaft* 28 (1971): 119-33.

————. "Mendelssohns Kompositionsweise 2: Weitere Vergleiche zwischen den Skizzen und der Letztfassung des Violinkonzerts op. 64." In *Das ProblemMendelssohn*, edited by Carl Dahlhaus, Regensburg: Bosse, 1974.

Seaton, Douglass "A Study of a Collection of Mendelssohn's Sketches and Other Autograph Material: Deutsche Staatsbibliothek Berlin Mus. Ms. Autogr. Mendelssohn 19." Ph.D. diss., Columbia University, 1977.

Todd, R. Larry. *Mendelssohn, the Hebrides and Other Overtures: A Midsummer Night's Dream, Calm Sea and Prosperous Voyage, The Hebrides*. Cambridge: Cambridge University Press, 1993.

————. *Mendelssohn's Musical Education: a Study and Edition of his Exercises in Composition: Oxford Bodleian ms. Margaret Deneke Mendelssohn C. 43*. Cambridge: Cambridge University Press, 1983.

Vitercik, Gregory John. *The Early Works of Felix Mendelssohn: a Study in the Romantic Sonata Style*. Philadelphia: Gordon and Breach, 1992.

Biographies

Köhler, Karl-Heinz. *Felix Mendelssohn Bartholdy*. Leipzig: Reclam, 1966.

Konold, Wulf. *Felix Mendelssohn Bartholdy und seine Zeit*. Laaber: Laaber, 1984.

Stresemann, Wolfgang. *Eine Lanze für Felix Mendelssohn*. Berlin: Stapp, 1984.

Lampadius, Wilhelm Adolf. *Felix Mendelssohn Bartholdy. Ein Gesamtbild seines Leben und Schaffens*. Leipzig, Leuckart, 1886.

Radcliffe, Philip. *Mendelssohn*. London: J. M. Dent, 1954.

Werner, Eric. *Mendelssohn: A New Image of the Composer and His Age*. New York: Free Press of Glencoe, 1963.

Wolff, Ernst. *Felix Mendelssohn Bartholdy*. Berlin: Verlagsgesellschaft für Literatur und Kunst, 1906.

The Oratorio in the Early- and Mid-Nineteenth Century

Hopkins Porter, Cecelia. "The New Public and the Reordering of the Musical Establishment: The Lower Rhine Music Festivals, 1818-67. " *19th-Century Music* 3/3 (March 1980): 211-24.

Sattler, W. "Die Bedeutung der Singakademie zu Berlin für die liturgisch-musikalische Entwicklung Schleiermachers." *Zeitschrift für Musikwissenschaft* 1 (1918-19), 165-76

Schering, Arnold. *Geschichte des Oratoriums*. Leipzig: 1911. Reprint, Hildesheim: 1968.

Smither, Howard E. *A History of the Oratorio*. Vol. 3, *The Oratorio in the Classical Era*. Chapel Hill: University of North Carolina Press, 1987.

Sulzer, Johann Georg. *Allgemeine Theorie der schönen Künste*. Leipzig: Weidmannsche Buchhandlung, 1793; reprint Hildesheim: Olms, 1967.

Index

About the Author

Siegwart Reichwald (B.M., University of South Carolina; M.M. and Ph.D., Florida State University) is an assistant professor of music history/musicology at Palm Beach Atlantic College in West Palm Beach, FL; he also directs the Palm Beach Atlantic Symphony there, a college/community orchestra. Dr. Reichwald's area of specialization is nineteenth-century music; he has presented papers on compositions by Felix Mendelssohn, Fanny Hensel, Robert and Clara Schumann, and Ludwig van Beethoven. He has, however, also done extensive research, presented papers, and published an article on topics of the Renaissance and the twentieth century. Dr. Reichwald is an active church musician and served as Music Director at the Independent Presbyterian Church in Savannah, Georgia (1993-95).